JOHN BUTT was Regius Professor of Rhetoric and English literature at Edinburgh from 1959 until his death in November, 1965. He was educated at Shrewsbury School and Merton College, Oxford, and he taught at the University of London (1930-1946), Newcastle (1946-1959) and, as Visiting Professor, at the University of California (1952) and Yale (1962). From 1932 to 1965 he was General Editor of the Twickenham edition of Pope's poetry. He also edited *The Review of English Studies* (1947-1954). His publications include: *Pope's Taste in Shakespeare* (1936); *Augustans and Romantics* (1940); *Fielding* (1954); and *Dickens at Work* (1957, with K. Tillotson).

THE AUGUSTAN AGE

JOHN BUTT

The Norton Library
W · W · NORTON & COMPANY · INC ·
NEW YORK

W. W. Norton & Company, Inc. is also the publisher of
The Norton Anthology of English Literature, edited by M. H.
Abrams, Robert M. Adams, David Daiches, E. Talbot Donaldson,
George H. Ford, Samuel Holt Monk, and Hallett Smith; *The American
Tradition in Literature,* edited by Sculley Bradley, Richmond
Croom Beatty, and E. Hudson Long; *World Masterpieces,* edited
by Maynard Mack, Kenneth Douglas, Howard E. Hugo, Bernard
M. W. Knox, John C. McGalliard, P. M. Pasinetti, and René Wellek;
and the paperbound Norton Critical Editions—authoritative texts,
together with the leading critical interpretations, of *Adventures of
Huckleberry Finn, The Ambassadors, Crime and Punishment, Gulliver's Travels, Hamlet, Heart of Darkness, Henry IV, Part 1,
Madame Bovary, The Red Badge of Courage, The Scarlet Letter,* and
Wuthering Heights.

CONTENTS

PREFACE TO THIRD EDITION

THE 'Notes for Further Reading' have been expanded and brought up to date, but in other respects the text of this edition, apart from a few corrections, remains essentially the same as in earlier editions.

J. B.

PREFACE TO FIRST EDITION

THIS book is not intended as a short history of English Literature of the Augustan Age. I have limited myself to the work of a few writers of paramount interest, because I think that the student for whom this book is written will wish to start in this way. Eventually he will want to read the work of the minor writers of the age, but first he will want to know what such men as Dryden, Swift, Pope, and a few others have to say. What they wrote was directed to their contemporaries with whose thoughts and actions most of them were immediately concerned. I have therefore attempted to set them against the background of the age in which they lived, and in so doing I have incidentally discussed the writings of many lesser men as well.

The Augustan Age used to be called the Age of Prose and Reason. Of what was meant by reason I have something to say; but though Addison, Swift, and Johnson are discussed at some length, I have paid less attention to the prose than would have been expected sixty years ago. The important developments which took place in novel and philosophical writing have been left, apart from incidental references, to other volumes in this series; and nothing will be found in this book about Augustan drama. This rigorous method of selection has allowed me to concentrate on what was once so much despised, the poetry of the time and, incidentally, the critical theory that supported it. In the poetry we can clearly see the temper of the age, the persuasions and implicit beliefs of the cultivated

Augustan Englishman. But though this approach to the age through its poetry is pleasing and legitimate, and may help in turn towards a better understanding of the poetry, it should not be allowed to become an end in itself, and to deflect us from recognizing the peculiar yet varied poetical achievements which this book attempts to expound.

In an appendix I have made a list of books and articles for further reading which will also serve, I hope, as an acknowledgment of some of the help I have received. To my friends Dr. Harold Brooks, Professor Louis Landa, Dr. Angus Macdonald, and Professor Geoffrey Tillotson I owe a more particular debt. They have each read one chapter or more in typescript, and from their searching comments I have derived the greatest benefit.

J. B.

CHAPTER I

DRYDEN

'HE found it brick and he left it marble'. These are the words which Dr. Johnson chose to describe what Dryden did for English poetry, and they express the view widely held in the eighteenth century that Dryden stood at the beginning of a new epoch in English Literature. Dryden himself would not have disagreed. He recognized, as all his contemporaries recognized, that the restoration of Charles II in the year 1660 marked the beginning of a new era in the history of poetry and drama as clearly as in constitutional and ecclesiastical history, and he was fond of comparing the achievements of his own age with those of the Elizabethans, 'the Giant Race before the Flood', as he called them. The conclusion of a successful play might tempt him to exclaim that

> Wit's now ariv'd to a more high degree;
> Our native Language more refin'd and free;
> Our Ladies and our men now speak more wit
> In conversation, than those Poets writ;

but looking back at the end of his life on the achievements of the age, he told his young friend, Congreve, that he was dissatisfied:

> Our Age was cultivated thus at length,
> But what we gain'd in Skill we lost in Strength.
> Our Builders were with Want of Genius curst;
> The second Temple was not like the first.

There is much in post-Restoration literature to remind the reader of 'the Giant Race before the Flood'. The Restoration poets had not forgotten the lessons of Ben Jonson nor the practice of Cowley; and the Jacobean tradition in Restoration

drama is stronger than nineteenth-century critics, with their
eyes fixed on French models, were prepared to admit. For all
that, the gulf, which separated the two ages and seemed so
obvious to Dryden and his successors as they contrasted the
products of the untutored genius of the earlier age with their
own more 'correct' taste, did in fact exist. The Civil Wars and
the period of Puritan supremacy had lasted eighteen years, long
enough to permit an even greater break in tradition than actually
occurred. Of the older writers whose eminence was recognized
by their contemporaries, two were to live in retirement for the
rest of their days, Cowley from temperamental choice, Milton
because he was too deeply committed to the principles and
policy of the earlier régime to compromise with its successor.
Thus, since only Davenant, Waller, and Denham survived
from the older generation to write for the new, the opportunity
lay with the younger men.

'Our native Language more refin'd and free'. Dryden's
phrase draws attention to the twofold achievement of the
Augustan Age. 'Refinement' suggests a process of selection and
cultivation, the process by which the best breeds of garden
flowers and fruit have been produced from the wildness of the
state of nature. The Augustans would have accepted this
analogy to describe the distinction between their work and the
work of the Elizabethans, who seemed to rely for their effects
solely upon the untutored force of their imagination. Such
criticism had been heard in the Elizabethan Age itself. Ben
Jonson had told Drummond 'That Shakspear wanted Arte',
and a famous passage in *Discoveries* shows us something of
what he meant:

I remember, the Players have often mentioned it as an honour to
Shakespeare, that in his writing, (whatsoever he penn'd) hee never
blotted out line. My answer hath beene, would he had blotted a
thousand. . . . Hee . . . had an excellent *Phantsie*; brave notions, and
gentle expressions: wherein hee flow'd with that facility, that some-
time it was necessary he should be stop'd: *Sufflaminandus erat;* as
Augustus said of *Haterius.* His wit was in his owne power; would the
rule of it had beene so too. Many times hee fell into those things,
could not escape laughter: As when hee said in the person of *Caesar,*

one speaking to him; *Caesar thou dost me wrong*. Hee replyed: *Caesar did never wrong, but with just cause:* and such like ; which were ridiculous.

'Arte', then, involved the labour of the file, the rejection of superfluities, of puns, irrelevant witticisms, and other quirks of fancy, the rejection of all that failed to reach the highest standard. And how could that standard be reached except by cultivating a taste for the best models of classical antiquity and submitting to the rules for composition in the various kinds of literary art discovered by those critics who had most carefully studied the ancients?

Art was also understood to involve selecting an appropriate 'diction' for poetry. The word 'diction', significantly enough, is first used by Dryden,[1] but the thing had long been recognized. We need go no further back than 1579 to find Spenser deliberately choosing 'old and vnwonted words' for *The Shepheardes Calender* and being commended for his choice by his commentator, E.K. Spenser may be said to have had a theory of diction; so had Donne and his followers, such poets as George Herbert, Crashaw, and Cleveland, who in their choice of words consciously blended the colloquial and the bizarre to give the effect of immediacy to their poetry. But the poetic intentions of the Augustans involved new theories of selection. Each poetic kind—the epic, the ode, the satire—was recognized as having its own appropriate diction. The diction for which eighteenth-century poetry has often been censured was the diction considered proper for pastoral and georgic poetry; it was never used for moral and satiric poetry, where at first sight questions of diction would scarcely seem to enter at all. As we shall see, the sources of these types of diction are quite different. Yet the best poets in each kind consciously used the same process, a process of refinement of their raw materials by rigorous selection.

But Dryden claimed that the language of the Augustans was not only more 'refin'd' than the Elizabethans' language; it was

[1]'There appears in every part of Horace's diction, or (to speak English) in all his Expressions, a kind of noble and bold Purity. His Words are chosen with as much exactness as Virgils; but there seems to be a greater Spirit in them'. Preface to *Sylvae*, 1685.

more 'free' as well. 'Refin'd and free': the ideal bears a wider application than the use of language. It is no good learning refinement of thought, speech, and bearing, unless at the same time your manner is easy. 'To preserve the true character of Homer's style', Pope wrote in the Postscript to his translation of the *Odyssey*, 'great pains have been taken to be easy and natural'; it sounds like a paradox; but Pope was expressing a widely felt belief when he wrote in the *Essay on Criticism:*

> True ease in writing comes from art, not chance,
> As those move easiest who have learn'd to dance:

and it is Pope again who provides us, in a character of his friend Lord Bolingbroke, with a succinct statement of the ideal which most writers aimed at:

> Correct with spirit, eloquent with ease.

It was this Olympian ease and urbanity which Dryden achieved and which distinguished him in the eyes of his contemporaries from his Elizabethan predecessors. At the Restoration Dryden was twenty-nine years old, and had published little to justify prophecy of future fame. Some verses on the death of Lord Hastings, contributed to a memorial volume (1649), suggested that the schoolboy who wrote them was attracted by the 'conceited' style of Crashaw and Cleveland, and the stanzas written ten years later on Oliver Cromwell's death hinted at epic ambitions. These stanzas are described as 'heroic' and are written in the quatrain, which Davenant had chosen for his epic poem, *Gondibert*, published eight years earlier in 1651. To succeed in heroic poetry was the aim of every poet with high aspirations, for heroic poetry (to use Dryden's words) 'has ever been esteemed . . . the greatest work of human nature'. It was the form in which the ancients had excelled, and therefore the spirit of rivalry drove the moderns to attempt it and thus to justify their age. Furthermore, it was 'the most noble, the most pleasant, and the most instructive way of writing in verse', Dryden thought, 'and withal the highest pattern of human life'. It is not surprising, therefore, that Dryden should be found exercising himself in the recognized heroic measure both in the Cromwell stanzas and in *Annus Mirabilis* (1667), his first long narrative poem written in reply to a series of seditious pamphlets, as was recently shown,[1] to explain that the disasters of 1666—a consuming plague, followed by an even more consuming fire and a war which, if not disastrous, was proving most expensive—were trials, not judgments, and would help to bind a loyal people more devotedly to the Sovereign who shared their sufferings.

The moment was admirably chosen, the plan clearly conceived and brilliantly executed. On this evidence alone Dryden had the makings of an astute political tactician. But he could never give his mind wholly to politics. Beside the political journalist sat the man of letters making out of current events an occasion for literary exercise. '*I have called my Poem* Historical, *not Epick*', he writes in 'An Account of the Ensuing Poem', the first of many critical prefaces to his works, '*though both the Actions and Actors are as much Heroick as any Poem can contain*'. But even if there is something wanting to an epic poem both in construction and length, *Annus Mirabilis* is, nevertheless, heroic poetry on an heroic theme. Dryden had succeeded in making a political emergency serve as occasion for an exercise in heroic writing.

A similar opportunity occurred fourteen years later. Perhaps in recognition of the astuteness of Dryden's defence of the Crown in *Annus Mirabilis*, Charles II had appointed him Poet Laureate on Davenant's death in 1668 and Historiographer Royal in 1670. In which capacity Dryden wrote *Absalom and Achitophel* need not concern us, but it is generally accepted that the suggestion for the poem came from the King, who probably told Dryden what line to take and what support he needed from his laureate-historiographer in securing the conviction of Shaftesbury (Achitophel), the leader of the Whig party. As in 1667 so in 1681, Dryden turned a political emergency to literary effect. A lampoon on Shaftesbury might have served the purpose, but Dryden's epic ambitions were still unfulfilled and here was an opportunity for further exercise in heroic poetry. The French poet, Boileau, had recently shown

[1]Edward N. Hooker, 'The purpose of Dryden's *Annus Mirabilis*', *Huntington Library Quarterly* (1946), x. i. 49ff.

in his famous poem, *Le Lutrin* (1674), that the majesty of the heroic can be finely mixed with the venom of satire; and though Boileau's subject was essentially trivial, his example may have provided Dryden with the hint he required.

The theme Dryden chose, or the King suggested—we cannot be quite certain which—was the theme of temptation. An arch-rebel (Shaftesbury-Achitophel), who suffers from a turbulent pride of intellect and will brook no authority, attempts to lure an inexperienced young man (Monmouth-Absalom) from his allegiance to the appointed order in the State. The theme oddly resembles the theme of *Paradise Lost*, published fourteen years earlier, and Dryden may have recognized the similarity: ''*tis no more a wonder that he* [Absalom] *withstood not the temptations of* Achitophel', he writes in his preface, '*than it was for* Adam *not to have resisted the two Devils, the Serpent and the Woman*'; and as for Achitophel, Dryden is charitable enough to hope, with Origen, that the Devil himself may be saved. Whether or not Dryden was aware of that resemblance, he must have regarded the characters of the rebel angels and the orations made in the second book of *Paradise Lost* as authority for similar character sketches and similar orations in *Absalom and Achitophel*.

Certainly Dryden aimed at the majesty of heroic poetry in *Absalom and Achitophel*, nor was he likely to forget that an epic poet should instruct. He attempts in this poem and in its sequel, *The Medall* (1682), to interpret events in the light of political theory. Dryden's generation had learned from Hobbes's *Leviathan* (1651) that men, growing weary of a state of nature 'where every man is Enemy to every man' and man's life was 'solitary, poore, nasty, brutish, and short', had contracted to surrender the right of governing themselves to a sovereign. In return, the Sovereign had promised to secure peace at home and defence from enemies of the State. This contract was supposed to be irrevocable. It passed from king to king in succession, and was reaffirmed in the coronation oath. In Dryden's eyes, Shaftesbury was attempting to destroy the contract by investing more power in the people:

He preaches to the Crowd that Pow'r is lent,
But not convey'd to Kingly Government;
That Claimes successive bear no binding force;
That Coronation Oaths are things of course;
Maintains the Multitude can never err;
And sets the People in the Papal Chair.
The reason's obvious; *Int'rest never lyes;*
The most have still their Int'rest in their eyes;
The pow'r is always theirs, and pow'r is ever wise.

These lines are taken from *The Medall*, where Dryden's teaching is more explicit. But in *Absalom and Achitophel* we also find the theory of contract debated and the penalty of revoking it—no less than anarchy—clearly stated (I. 409–16; 759–80); anarchy, that chaos which Dryden, as well as Shakespeare and his contemporaries knew would follow 'when degree is suffocate'.[1]

No one could accuse Dryden of neglecting an epic writer's duty to teach in this, his nearest approximation to an epic. The epic itself was fated never to be written. In his old age he mentioned that he would have chosen for his subject either King Arthur conquering the Saxons, a subject which Milton also had left unwritten and was to fall into the hands of Sir Richard Blackmore, or Edward, the Black Prince, subduing Spain. 'But', Dryden continues, 'being encouraged only with fair words by King Charles II, my little salary ill paid, and no prospect of a future subsistence, I was then discouraged in the beginning of my attempt; and now age has overtaken me, and want . . . has wholly disabled me'.

It is useless to speculate upon what Charles II's niggardliness has lost us. Dryden's remarks upon the epic form in his 'Discourse concerning the Original and Progress of Satire' might lead us to think that the conventional epic devices, already tabulated by generations of critics, would have been ingeniously adapted to the conditions of his day, for Dryden was always at his happiest when attempting to solve a literary problem of that kind. He enjoys discovering what life can be

[1] It is interesting to notice that three years earlier Dryden had remodelled Ulysses' great exposition of 'degree' in a version of Shakespeare's *Troilus and Cressida*.

breathed into an old convention, or reconciling (as in *All for Love*) the freedom of Elizabethan dramatic construction with the strictness of neo-classical form. Indeed, he might have claimed that in *Absalom and Achitophel*, and perhaps even in the burlesque fragment *Mac Flecknoe*, he had breathed new life into the epic, had made the satiric version of it serve the needs of a later and less heroic age.

The heroic measure in these approximations to heroic poetry was no longer the quatrain: it was the couplet. Dryden had been impelled to make the change by the experiments in heroic tragedy which had engaged him in the years intervening between *Annus Mirabilis* and *Absalom and Achitophel*. Not only would the quatrain have been a quite unsuitable measure for drama, but Dryden was now veering round to think that the 'excellence and dignity' of the couplet as used by Waller and Denham, who 'first showed us to conclude the sense most commonly in distichs', was the most suitable form of verse for heroic poetry wherein Nature is represented 'wrought up to a higher pitch'.

Dryden admitted in later years that his genius never much inclined him to the drama, a view from which no subsequent critic has been able to dissent. No doubt he reflected that the theatre was the plaything of Charles II and his court, and that a man of letters might make a living there. Certainly it was as a man of letters that he applied himself to playwriting, and not as a dramatist, for while he wrote for the stage his head was full of his epic ambitions. His intention was to develop a new type of tragedy, an heroic play, from hints left by Davenant and Corneille. As he experimented, his ideas grew clearer and he was able to state in an 'Essay of Heroic Plays' prefixed to the most famous of them, *The Conquest of Granada* (1672), that an heroic play ought to be an imitation in little of an heroic poem. To us it may seem an odd conclusion to reach, and one which could not have been reached by a man entirely absorbed in the problems of dramatic form; but no critic of that day would have disputed the virtual identity of tragedy and epic. Hobbes had said as much in a letter addressed to Davenant, published with *Gondibert* (1651):

For the Heroique Poem narrative, such as yours, is called an *Epique Poem*. The Heroique Poem Dramatique is *Tragedy* . . . The Figure therefore of an Epique Poem and of a Tragedy ought to be the same, for they differ no more but in that they are pronounced by one or many Persons,

an opinion Dryden was to echo in his *Essay of Dramatic Poesy* (1668). From this it would follow that the first business of the tragic dramatist, as of the epic poet, is to teach, to insinuate a precept of morality into the audience (to use Dryden's words). Thus the 'moral' of *The Conquest of Granada* was derived from the Iliad, namely 'that union preserves a commonwealth, and discord destroys it'. Similarly the characters are planned to be of epic stature—Almanzor was said to be modelled on Homer's Achilles and Tasso's Rinaldo—and even epic similes and epic narrative are not considered out of place. So much deference Dryden was ready to pay to critical precept. But in his interpretation of the critical 'rules' he was always liberal, always ready to let practical experience permit an extension of them. So we find in these heroic plays that though much is epic (and consequently non-dramatic) in manner, there is also much to appeal to the contemporary love of exotic display and extravagant emotionalism. In the conflict between Love and Honour, so monotonously presented in one play after another, the issue is never seriously in doubt: all is for love, and the world is well lost. The heroic plays are not so much tragedy as opera *manqué*. But one thing at least Dryden achieved by his dramatic experiments. He revealed the immense resonance of which the heroic couplet was capable, its variety of speed and of cadence, and in those capital prologues and epilogues he showed to what varied uses it could be put. We know that on at least one occasion on the Elizabethan stage Shakespeare's *Julius Caesar* was concluded with a jig. It is in that tradition that Dryden composed this merry epilogue for Nell Gwynn to speak at the end of *Tyrannic Love* (1669).

Spoken by MRS. ELLEN *when she was to be carried off dead by the Bearers.*

To the Bearer: Hold! are you mad? you damn'd, confounded Dog!
     I am to rise, and speak the Epilogue.

To the Audience: I come, kind Gentlemen, strange news to tell ye ;
            I am the Ghost of poor departed *Nelly*.
            Sweet Ladies, be not frighted: I'le be civil;
            I'm what I was, a little harmless Devil.
            For, after death, we Sprights have just such Natures,
            We had, for all the World, when humane Creatures;
            And, therefore, I, that was an Actress here,
            Play all my Tricks in Hell, a Goblin there.
            Gallants, look to 't, you say there are no Sprights;
            But I'll come dance about your Beds at nights;
            And faith you'll be in a sweet kind of taking,
            When I surprise you between sleep and waking.
            To tell you true, I walk, because I dye
            Out of my Calling, in a Tragedy.
            O Poet, damn'd dull Poet, who could prove
            So senseless, to make *Nelly* dye for Love!
            Nay, what's yet worse, to kill me in the prime
            Of *Easter*-term, in Tart and Cheese-cake time!
            I'le fit the Fopp; for I'le not one word say,
            T''excuse his godly, out of fashion Play;
            A Play, which, if you dare but twice sit out,
            You'll all be slander'd, and be thought devout.
            But, farewel, Gentlemen, make haste to me,
            I'm sure e're long to have your company.
            As for my Epitaph when I am gone,
            I'le trust no Poet, but will write my own,
            Here *Nelly* lies, who, though she lived a Slater'n,
            Yet dy'd a Princess, acting in *S. Cathar'n*.

During the last twenty years of his life Dryden was much
occupied with poetical translation. The problem he set himself
was how to make his author 'speak that kind of English which
he would have spoken had he lived in England and had written
to this age'. He found two schools of thought amongst his
immediate predecessors. Some translators, like Ben Jonson,
aimed at metaphrase, 'or turning an author word by word, and
line by line, from one language to another'. But, says Dryden,
'too faithfully is, indeed, pedantically . . .'tis almost impossible
to translate verbally, and well, at the same time'. Others, like
Denham and Cowley, preferred imitation, 'where the translator . . . assumes the liberty, not only to vary from the words

and sense, but to forsake them both as he sees occasion; and taking only some general hints from the original, to run division on the ground-work, as he pleases'. But this, as Dryden objects, is scarcely to translate at all. Instead he attempted to steer a middle course in which, though the sense of the author must be sacred and inviolable, such liberties with his words may be taken as will make him write good modern English. Above all the spirit of the original must be preserved, and the translator must take care that his genius conforms to his author's. Dryden admitted that he transgressed the rules he gave, and at times his renderings, like those of the Elizabethan verse translators before him, are dangerously close to 'imitation'. '*Quas ferat et referat sollers ancilla tabellas*', writes Ovid in the nineteenth elegy of his second book. Dryden cannot resist a modern parallel:

> An Orange-wench wou'd tempt thy Wife abroad;
> Kick her, for she's a Letter-bearing Bawd;

but there is a raciness in the rendering which every reader will forgive, just as he will unhesitatingly overlook whatever licence Dryden took in his noble version of the twenty-ninth ode of the third book of *Horace*. This was Lord Rochester's 'darling in the Latin', says Dryden, 'and I have taken some pains to make it my master-piece in English'. For that reason, he says, he attempted to translate it in Pindaric verse. The fashion for writing 'Pindaric' odes had been started in the previous generation by Cowley, who had attempted to show that the sublimity of Pindar, the enthusiastic vigour of his style, is best imitated in irregular verse.

The Pindaric Ode, as Cowley practised it in such odes as 'To Mr. Hobbes' and 'To the Royal Society', consisted of an indefinite number of stanzas containing an indefinite number of lines, the lines containing an indefinite number of stresses. 'This lax and lawless versification', wrote Dr. Johnson, one hundred years later, 'so much concealed the deficiencies of the barren and flattered the laziness of the idle, that it immediately overspread our books of poetry; all the boys and girls caught the pleasing fashion, and they that could do nothing else could

write like Pindar'. That is one way of looking at the fashion.
Looked at from another point of view, this fashion shows that,
in an age of respect for rule and classical precedent, there were
poets who believed they could snatch a grace beyond the reach
of art if their inspiration were sufficiently sublime. As we shall
see, they were to receive encouragement from the increased
attention paid to the Greek critic Longinus after the publication
of Boileau's translation of περὶ ὕψους (Concerning the Sublime)
in 1674.

Dryden's attitude to the new fashion is characteristic of his
poetical 'trimming'. He enjoyed the boldness of the experiment,
but he also had a respect for rule and would probably have
agreed with Sir Joshua Reynolds's dictum that 'as . . . art
shall advance, its powers will be still more and more fixed by
rules'[1]; thus while he relished the latitude which Pindaric
verse afforded, he admitted that it had not been 'considered'
and 'cultivated' enough. He will not go so far as to prescribe
precise rules for varying the number of stresses in the lines
of a stanza, since 'the ear must preside, and direct the judgment
to the choice of numbers: without the nicety of this, the
harmony of Pindaric verse can never be complete; the cadency
of one line must be a rule to that of the next; and the sound of
the former must slide gently into that which follows, without
leaping from one extreme into another. It must be done like
the shadowings of a picture, which fall by degrees into a darker
colour'.[2]

The success of this experiment prompted Dryden to use the
form for original verse. In the following month (February, 1685),
he chose the pindaric for an official ode (*Threnodia Augustalis*)
on the death of Charles II, and in the following year for an ode
to the memory of the poetess, Anne Killigrew: more striking
is his use of the form in the two odes for music written for the
annual celebrations of the Musical Society on St. Cecilia's Day,
A Song for St. Cecilia's Day (1687) and *Alexander's Feast* (1697).
Later critics have sometimes complained of the glittering

[1] *Discourse*, No. 6.
[2] Preface to *Sylvae*, 1685 (Dryden's *Essays*, ed. Ker [Oxford 1900] i.
26).

rhetoric of these odes, forgetting that the odes were designed
for music, that the composer would welcome emphatic repetitions, and that it lies in the power of music to naturalize a too
bold expression in verse. The composer needs, and from
Dryden he receives, a stimulating variety of verse rhythms;
'the softness and variety of numbers' is Dryden's phrase in his
preface to the opera *Albion and Albanius* (1685), where he adds,
'the chief secret is the choice of words . . . not elegancy of
expression, but propriety of sound, to be varied according to
the nature of the subject'. It was in following these principles
that he wrote such verses as those describing the effect of the
trumpet, drum, flute, and violin in the first St. Cecilia ode.
This is not to say that these odes sacrifice intellectual content
to rhythmical virtuosity. Dryden cannot resist a mild satiric
stroke at Alexander's expense, when

> Sooth'd with the Sound the King grew vain;
> Fought all his Battails o'er again;
> And thrice he routed all his Foes, and thrice he slew the slain.

Similarly in *The Secular Masque* (1700), the last words he
wrote for music, he finds no difficulty in representing in lyric
measure what we may take to be one view of the Civil Wars
current in the Restoration courts:

> *Momus to Mars—*
> Thy Sword within the Scabbard keep,
> And let Mankind agree;
> Better the World were fast asleep,
> Than kept awake by thee.
> The Fools are only thinner,
> With all our Cost and Care;
> But neither side a winner,
> For Things are as they were.

It is impossible to overlook Dryden's interest in the making
of good verses, for there is scarcely one of his critical prefaces
without some discussion of the literary problem he had set
himself in the ensuing work, the difficulties he had encountered
and the way he had overcome them. Even the exposition of his
religious faith in *Religio Laici* (1682) concludes with some

couplets on the type of verse he had adopted and his reason for
adopting it:

> Thus have I made my own Opinions clear:
> Yet neither Praise expect, nor Censure fear:
> And this unpolish'd, rugged verse I chose;
> As fittest for Discourse, and nearest prose.

But we must beware of assuming, as some critics have done,
that because Dryden is persistently occupied with problems of
craftsmanship he is interested in nothing else. He was well
aware of what the thinkers and scholars of his day were doing,
and he reflects their work in his verses. In 1662 he was elected
a member of the Royal Society, his sponsor being his 'honour'd
friend' Walter Charleton, the author of several medical,
antiquarian, and philosophical tracts. To one of these, *Chorea
Gigantum* (1663), written to prove that Stonehenge was built
by the Danes, Dryden contributed some commendatory verses
infected by the elation of his fellow-members at the triumphs
of the New Philosophy. Just as Cowley in his 'Ode to Mr.
Hobbes' and Glanvill in *The Vanity of Dogmatizing* (1661) had
ridiculed the long stranglehold of Aristotle upon natural
philosophy, so Dryden (echoing Cowley) complains:

> The longest Tyranny that ever sway'd
> Was that wherein our Ancestors betray'd
> Their free-born Reason to the *Stagirite*,
> And made his Torch their universal Light.

In the conflict between the Ancients and the Moderns, there
is no doubt where Dryden stands:

> Had we still paid that homage to a *Name*,
> Which only God and *Nature* justly claim,
> The *Western* Seas had been our utmost bound,
> Where *Poets* still might dream the *Sun* was drown'd:

but now that we are released from that devitalizing respect for
Authority, we are in a fair way for making scientific progress:

> Among th' Assertors of free Reason's claim,
> Th' *English* are not the least in Worth, or Fame.
> The World to *Bacon* does not onely owe
> Its *present* Knowledge, but its *future* too . . .

The *Circling* streams, once thought but pools, of blood
(Whether Life's fewel or the Bodie's food)
From dark Oblivion *Harvey's* name shall save;
While *Ent*[1] keeps all the honour that he gave.

We should not make too much of a mere echo of what many were saying, nor indeed of Dryden's membership of the Royal Society which he allowed to lapse after three years. But it shows at least that he attended to what was being said, and understood its importance. 'Is it not evident', he makes Crites remark, in *An Essay of Dramatic Poesy* (1668), 'is it not evident, in these last hundred years (when the study of philosophy [i.e. natural science] has been the business of all the Virtuosi in Christendom), that almost a new Nature has been revealed to us?—that more errors of the school [i.e. of the 'schoolmen', Aristotle's followers in the Middle Ages] have been detected, more useful experiments in philosophy have been made, more noble secrets in optics, medicine, anatomy, astronomy, discovered, than in all those credulous and doting ages from Aristotle to us?—so true it is, that nothing spreads more fast than science, when rightly and generally cultivated'. It is a neat summary, and the more impressive for being put into the mouth of a speaker whose business in the dialogue is to defend the claims of the Ancients in Drama against those of the Moderns.

Not only was Dryden aware of trends in natural and (as we have seen) in political philosophy, he also reflects the conflict the 'new philosophy' had raised between Reason and Faith. The first important statement of his religious position is found in his poem *Religio Laici* (1682). The title recalls the title of Sir Thomas Browne's book, published forty years earlier and still a popular book in Dryden's day; and the two works have this much in common: they were written by men of sceptical disposition looking for a firmer foundation for their faith, trying to establish their positions, and stating their special difficulties. Dryden says he is an Anglican, but there is nothing to show that he is convinced of the Anglican position. For him, religious—or perhaps we should say, ecclesiastical—issues were

[1]The physician who vindicated Harvey's discovery of the circulation of the blood.

inevitably bound up with politics. We have seen him in *Absalom and Achitophel* and *The Medall* using Hobbes's arguments to show that civil peace depends upon the king's supremacy and upon an immutable succession to the throne which the theory of contract implies. It was just here that his objection, as an Anglican, to papists and dissenters lay. On the one hand he found the Jesuits claiming that the Pope has an infallible right over kings, and can by excommunication release their subjects from their obedience; on the other, he saw that dissenters never lacked a text from Scripture to permit them to rebel. Dryden was thus forced to conclude that if he were anything else but an Anglican he would be endangering the King's supremacy and, with it, that sublime conception of order or 'degree' upon which the peace of the realm depended. Another difficulty was equally topical. What amount of credit should be given to the Scriptures?[1] Can we assume, as Anglicans and Dissenters maintained, that they are generally intelligible to the powers of human reason and contain everything necessary to salvation? Certain Roman Catholic apologists contested the position. They could point to Father Simon's *Histoire Critique du Vieux Testament* (1678) to show that the Scriptures are not generally intelligible nor in any literal sense the word of God, and they had no difficulty in showing that Protestants seemed to interpret the Scriptures as they liked and to read into them whatever they wanted. Dryden, whose young friend Henry Dickinson had translated Father Simon's book, shows in *Religio Laici* that he was much impressed by this apologetic, and he spends thirty lines (ll. 252–81) in sympathetic exposition. The conclusion he reaches at the end of his exposition indicates that, though nominally Anglican, he is already half-way to the Roman faith:

> Such an *Omniscient* Church we wish indeed;
> 'Twere worth *Both Testaments*, and cast in the *Creed*.

But in 1682 Dryden was content to think that the Roman Catholics were too confident in what they held. He preferred

[1] The subject is fully treated by L. I. Bredvold in *The Intellectual Milieu of John Dryden* (Ann Arbor, 1934).

to believe that the Scriptures are clearly intelligible wherever it is essential. Wherever else, we need a commentary; and we must consult, not our reason, but ancient tradition and the writings of the Fathers. *Not our reason:* that is significant of Dryden's sceptical, fideistic position. The Anglican Church had always been willing to assert the claims of reason to judge in religious matters; but though the Roman Church also maintained that there are perfectly good rational arguments to support the faith, unofficial Roman apologists were in the habit of disputing Reason's competence to decide in these matters, and Dryden, 'naturally inclined to Scepticism in Philosophy', had been listening to their arguments. *Religio Laici* confirms this. Far from asserting the competence of Reason, Dryden prefers to depreciate it; and it may be noticed that he gives his depreciation a political colour:

> And after hearing what our Church can say,
> If still our Reason runs another way,
> That private Reason 'tis more Just to curb,
> Than by Disputes the publick Peace disturb.

Three years after the poem was published, Charles II died and a Roman Catholic succeeded to the throne. Soon after, we hear of Dryden attending Mass. Naturally it would be said that self-interest urged his conversion, but Dryden repudiated the charge in *The Hind and the Panther* (1687; iii. 221 ff.), and examination of *Religio Laici* should force us to admit that his repudiation carries conviction. The political issue which had worried him at the time of writing *Religio Laici* had been removed by James II's succession; and as for the difficulty of scriptural interpretation, Dryden's position in *The Hind and the Panther* shows but a logical development from the already Romish position of the earlier poem. The sceptical, fideistic background of the two poems is the same. In *Religio Laici*, Dryden had wished for an omniscient church: now he has found one and deplores the lack of innate authority in the church he has left (i. 452–88). Dryden's resolution of the conflict between Faith and the evidence of Reason and the Senses will not satisfy everyone, but there is personal conviction expressed in the following lines which show that he could be inspired to write by things other than an interest in making good verses:

> My thoughtless youth was wing'd with vain desires,
> My manhood, long misled by wandring fires,
> Follow'd false lights; and when their glimps was gone,
> My pride struck out new sparkles of her own.
> Such was I, such by nature still I am,
> Be Thine the glory and be mine the shame.
> Good life be now my task: my doubts are done,
> (What more could fright my faith, than Three in One?)
> Can I believe eternal God could lye
> Disguis'd in mortal mold and infancy?
> That the great Maker of the world could dye?
> And after that trust my imperfect sense
> Which calls in question his omnipotence?
> Can I my reason to my faith compell,
> And shall my sight, and touch, and taste rebell?
> Superiour faculties are set aside,
> Shall their subservient organs be my guide?
> Then let the moon usurp the rule of day,
> And winking tapers show the sun his way;
> For what my senses can themselves perceive
> I need no revelation to believe.[1]

Dryden, then, exhibits an interest in a wide range of intellectual activity and in a wide range of literary forms. But above all he is interested in experiment, in exploring the frontier regions of poetry, prose, and drama, those regions where satire is near to epic, and epic is near to tragedy, and where literary criticism or a familiar letter, or a tale from Ovid or Boccaccio might be turned into verse or into 'the other harmony of prose'. We might say he was weak in imaginative poetry if we forgot the opening lines of *Religio Laici* and the concluding verses of 'To the Memory of Mr. John Oldham', or in love poetry if we forgot the fourth act of *Aurengzebe:* we could never forget how strong he is in the poetry of statement and declamation. No doubt it was such passages as Achitophel's great address to Absalom (ll. 230 ff.) and the opening of his

---

[1] *The Hind and the Panther*, i. 72–92.

translation of Juvenal's tenth satire, that Gerard Manley Hopkins had in mind when he wrote to Bridges:

I can scarcely think of you not admiring Dryden without, I may say, exasperation. . . . What is there in Dryden? Much, but above all this: he is the most masculine of our poets; his style and his rhythms lay the strongest stress of all our literature on the naked thew and sinew of the English language.

CHAPTER II

THE NEW AGE

'Tis well an old Age is out
And time to begin a new.

WITH these words Dryden dismissed the seventeenth century
in the last poem he wrote. The change from the old age to the
new was not so abrupt as Dryden seems to have wished; yet if
he had lived for another fifteen years he might have detected
some difference not merely in manners and literary taste but
in climate of opinion as well; for the intellectual problems which
had troubled the minds of his contemporaries were slowly being
resolved.

Seventeenth-century thought had been marked by a distaste
for Authority and for the quotation of ancient precedents. This
is evident in Milton's complaint that his adversaries' learning
and belief consisted only in 'marginal stuffings'. 'When they
have', he writes, 'like good sumpters laid ye down their horse-
load of citations and fathers at your door, with a rhapsody of
who and who were Bishops here or there, ye may take off their
packsaddles, their day's work is done, and episcopacy, as they
think, stoutly vindicated'. It is evident in Bacon's opinion that
'the overmuch credit . . . given unto authors in sciences . . . [is]
the principal cause that hath kept [sciences] low at a stay
without growth or advancement', an opinion echoed by Sir
Thomas Browne, Sprat, and Glanvill, who all recognized that
undue respect for the authority of the Ancients is the most
fruitful source of vulgar error. This distaste is evident in the
eight reasons Hobbes gave at the end of *Leviathan* for neglecting
'the Ornament of quoting ancient Poets, Orators, and Philosophers, contrary to the custome of late time'. It is evident,

above all, in the arguments of the defenders of the Moderns in their prolonged quarrel with the defenders of the Ancients both in this country and in France, arguments which amounted to declaring that men are no longer in leading strings to Greece and Rome, that modern achievements (especially in the natural sciences) have shown that the Moderns can stand on their own legs and be guided in the conduct of their affairs by the light of their own reason unclouded by respect for Ancient precedent. Even in the world of letters, where the respect for classical art forms and the rules for writing in those forms gave the defenders of the Ancients a decided advantage, critics could declare that the validity of the rules of art is derived from Reason rather than from Ancient Authority. Shakespeare, wrote Dennis in 1711, 'seems to have wanted nothing but Time and Leisure for Thought, to have found out those Rules of which he appears so ignorant'. He could have found them out because, as Pope claimed, they exist in Nature and are therefore discoverable by Reason. Such a claim could be made because seventeenth-century natural philosophy, culminating in the work of Sir Isaac Newton, had shown (in Dennis's words) that 'Nature is Order and Rule, and Harmony in the visible World' and is therefore comprehensible by Reason and subject to it.

Yet not every one would have agreed that Reason is a sufficient guide in the conduct of all human affairs. Though Sir Thomas Browne was active in rooting out errors derived from Ancient Authority, in Divinity he loved to keep the road and to teach his 'haggard and unreclaimed Reason to stoop unto the lure of Faith'; and though Dryden might not share Browne's solitary recreation of posing his apprehension with the involved enigmas and riddles of the Trinity, it is clear both from *Religio Laici* and *The Hind and the Panther* that he too used a *credo quia impossibile* to answer his rebellious Reason. Yet for Dryden's exact contemporary John Locke, as for Whichcote and his fellow Platonists, there was no such state of war between Faith and Reason: 'Faith', Locke declared, in *An Essay Concerning Humane Understanding* (1690), 'is nothing but a firm assent of the mind: which if it be regulated, as is our duty, cannot be afforded to any thing but upon good reason; and so cannot be opposite to it'. If, Locke continues, anything is revealed to us which is beyond the scope of knowledge, such as the resurrection of the dead, that is a matter of Faith, and Reason is concerned only to determine whether the revelation is divine; but of everything within the scope of knowledge, Reason is the sole judge.

Perhaps it was too readily assumed that every man can regulate his own reason; but that power being assumed, it is not difficult to see why the expert or 'specialist' should have begun to lose credit. For since every man is competent to decide, by reference to his own reason, on any point of natural or moral philosophy, every man becomes his own philosopher and the need for the expert vanishes. Bacon has been considered unduly presumptuous in taking all knowledge for his province. But few men at the end of the seventeenth century would have thought so, for there were several of their contemporaries who could make a similar claim. Sir William Petty (1623–87), for example, of whose achievements Evelyn gives a long account in his diary, was a Doctor of Physic, a designer of double-bottomed boats, and the delineator of the most accurate map of Ireland; he was an able statistician, and a wise counsellor in affairs of state; he had no equal in the superintendence of manufactures, in the improvement of trade, and in colonial government; and he had published ingenious deductions from the bills of mortality, a useful discourse on the manufacture of wool, and an inimitable paraphrase on the 104th Psalm in Latin verse. Evelyn himself was not far behind in accomplishments, with his knowledge of anatomy, forestry, architecture, town-planning, numismatics, and music. In an age when, as Dryden said, 'something new in philosophy and the mechanics is discovered almost every year', it must have seemed that there were no secrets which could be withheld from any man who used his observation and his reason. Even in the most abstruse provinces of knowledge the layman bid to replace the expert: we are told by the theologian Waterland, writing in 1723, that 'controversy on the Trinity was spread abroad among all ranks and degrees of men, and the Athanasian creed became the subject of common and ordinary conversation', and a recent historian has remarked that 'the House of Commons did not in the least consider its ignorance of Oriental languages, nor its imperfect acquaintance with patristic and historical studies, a barrier to its deliberation of ecclesiastical and theological questions'.

Something of the arrogant self-esteem with which Everyman contemplated himself in his new role is revealed in this ironical portrait from Berkeley's dialogue, *Alciphron* (1732):

Lysicles . . . smiled, and said he believed Euphranor had figured to himself philosophers in square caps and long gowns: but, thanks to these happy times, the reign of pedantry was over. Our philosophers, said he, are of a very different kind from those awkward students who think to come at knowledge by poring on dead languages, and old authors, or by sequestering themselves from the cares of the world to meditate in solitude and retirement. They are the best bred men of the age, men who know the world, men of pleasure, men of fashion, and fine gentlemen . . . *Crites*. The world, it seems, was long under a mistake about the way to knowledge, thinking it lay through a tedious course of academical education and study. But among the discoveries of the present age, one of the principal is the finding out that such a method doth rather retard and obstruct, than promote knowledge. *Alciphron*. Academical study may be comprised in two points, reading and meditation. Their reading is chiefly employed on ancient authors in dead languages: so that a great part of their time is spent in learning words; which, when they have mastered with infinite pains, what do they get by it but old and obsolete notions, that are now quite exploded and out of use? Then, as to their meditations, what can they possibly be good for? He that wants the proper materials of thought, may think and meditate for ever to no purpose: those cobwebs spun by scholars out of their brains being alike unserviceable, either for use or ornament. Proper ideas or materials are only to be got by frequenting good company. I know several gentlemen, who, since their first appearance in the world, have spent as much time in rubbing off the rust and pedantry of a College education, as they had done before in acquiring it. *Lysicles*. I'll undertake, a lad of fourteen, bred in the modern way, shall make a better figure, and be more considered in any drawing-room or assembly of polite people, than one of four and twenty, who hath lain by a long time at school or college. He shall say better things, in a better manner, and be more liked by good judges. *Euphranor*. Where doth he pick up all this improvement? *Crites*. Where our grave ancestors would never have looked for it, in a drawing-room, a coffee-house, a chocolate-house, at the tavern, or groom-porter's. In these and the like fashionable places of resort, it is the custom of polite persons to speak freely on all subjects, religious, moral, or political. So that a young gentleman who frequents them is in the way of hearing many instructive lectures, seasoned with wit and raillery, and uttered with spirit. Three or four sentences from a man of quality spoken with a good air, make more impression, and convey more knowledge, than a dozen dissertations in a dry academical way. *Euphranor*. There is then no method or course of studies in those places. *Lysicles*. None but an easy free conversation, which takes in every thing that offers, without any rule or reason.

But however wittily Berkeley might demur, the very form and style of his work show that the serious philosopher intended his books to be read, not merely by a group of experts in the subject, but by the generality of educated men.

Since all men, as was widely assumed, were equally endowed with the power of reasoning, it seemed to follow that when they reasoned on any given premises they ought to reach the same conclusion. That conclusion was believed to have universal value; it should appeal directly to everyone, irrespective of race and age: it should be simple, within the power of everyone to understand: and it should be the conclusion reached by earlier generations, since reason must work the same way in every period of history. When Pope said of Wit that it is 'Nature to advantage dress'd, What oft was thought but ne'er so well express'd', and when Johnson said of Gray's *Elegy* that it 'abounds with images which find a mirror in every mind, and with sentiments to which every bosom returns an echo', they were expressing the literary application of this belief— that the greatest art is that which is immediately understood and has the widest appeal, which avoids the expression of personal idiosyncrasy and notices 'general properties and large appearances' rather than what is too peculiar or particular.

This dislike of the 'particular' as opposed to what is true for all men at all times helps to explain why deism, or the principle of natural religion,[1] took so firm a hold on men's minds. While the benefits and general applicability of Christian morals were widely appreciated, the idea of a particular and partial revelation made in the person of Jesus to a small Eastern tribe proved something of a stumbling block. What is relevant to the salvation of all men, all men should surely have equal opportunities of enjoying. Attempts were therefore made to circumvent the difficulty, in one way by trying to show, like Matthew Tindal, that Christianity is as old as the Creation and that the Gospel is but a republication of the religion of nature, or in another by devising a creed out of what only is common to all religions of the world. The lowest common multiple would be a creed simple, universal, and reasonable. Alciphron describes the process and indicates where such a process must end:

First, I must acquaint you [Berkeley makes him say] that having applied my mind to contemplate the idea of truth, I discovered it to be of a stable, permanent, and uniform nature; not various and changeable, like modes or fashions, and things depending on fancy. In the next place, having observed several sects and subdivisions of sects espousing very different and contrary opinions, and yet all professing Christianity, I rejected those points wherein they differed, retaining only that which was agreed to by all; and so became latitudinarian. Having afterwards, upon a more enlarged view of things, perceived that Christians, Jews, and Mahometans had each their different systems of faith, agreeing only in the belief of one God, I became a deist. Lastly, extending my view to all the other various nations which inhabit this globe, and finding they agreed in no one point of faith, but differed one from another, as well as from the forementioned sects, even in the notion of a God, in which there is as great diversity as in the methods of worship, I thereupon became an atheist: it being my opinion that a man of courage and sense should follow his argument wherever it leads him, and that nothing is more ridiculous than to be a free thinker by halves.

[1]'BY *Natural Religion*, I understand the Belief of the Existence of a God, and the Sense and Practice of those Duties, which result from the knowledge, we, by our Reason, have of him, and of his Perfections; and of ourselves, and our own Imperfections; and of the Relation we stand in to him, and to our Fellow Creatures'. Tindal, *Christianity as Old as the Creation* (1730), p. 13.

Yet the appeal of the deists can still be felt to-day in an age striving to find common ground for action between all men of good will. For action was the end of the deists' intentions. They were speculative, not because speculation had an irresistible charm, but because it might lead to a surer ground for moral action. Since Christian teaching had been ineffectual in making men behave decently, they tried to find a stronger motive for decent behaviour in what would appeal to men's reasons instead of to their capacity for faith. So widespread was their influence that Butler, the most effective champion of orthodox Christianity, was constrained in his *Analogy of Religion* (1736) to demonstrate the reasonableness of Christian beliefs by showing that the difficulties in holding them are of exactly the same kind as the difficulties of natural religion, and that since the same handiwork is apparent in both dispensations, God is the author of both. Butler, that is to say, like Tillotson and Sherlock before him, grounds his work on the deists' position and works back from that to Christianity.

This, then, was the temper of the new age. If we persist in calling it 'The Age of Reason', we must not proceed to argue that it was an age in which the feelings were repressed and inspiration discounted. Rather it was an age which recognized that man's peculiar distinction was his power of reasoning upon the evidence which his senses supplied. It was an age which assumed that in reasoning power all men are and always have been equal, which constantly appealed to the common sense of mankind as evident in the work of Homer or Cicero as in that of the best of the Moderns, and which rejected as contrary to that common sense or agreement all subtleties of intellect ungrounded upon the evidence of the senses. It was an age which took a legitimate pride in modern discoveries based upon observation and reason, and which delighted to reflect that those discoveries had confirmed ancient beliefs in an orderly disposed rational universe, where each created thing had its allowed position and moved in its appointed sphere. It was an age which found fresh meaning in the words 'God saw everything that He had made, and behold, it was very good'; it was very good, it was in fact the best world God could have made, because it worked upon demonstrably rational principles. Such overpowering evidence of the universal validity of the rule of Reason was indeed sublime. The Age of Reason was also the Age of Rapture.

CHAPTER III

ADDISON

'Justness of Thought and Style, Refinement in Manners, good
Breeding, and Politeness of every kind'.
                    Shaftesbury, *A Letter Concerning Enthusiasm*, 1708.

THE spirit of the age can be compendiously studied in the pages
of *The Spectator*. In the tenth number of that periodical Addison
announced the policy which he and Steele were to follow. 'The
Spectator' was ambitious to have it said of him that he had
'brought Philosophy out of Closets and Libraries, Schools and
Colleges, to dwell in Clubs and Assemblies, at Tea-tables and
in Coffee-houses', and was resolved to recover his readers
'out of that desperate state of Vice and Folly' into which the
age was fallen. There was little new in this statement of policy,
and little new in the manner of carrying it out. Neither Addison
nor Steele could have afforded to attempt bold innovations,
for they were both leading the somewhat precarious existence
of politicians whose party was out of office. Steele, it is true,
was still Commissioner for Stamps at a salary of £300 a year,
but he had lost the Gazeteership a few months before *The
Spectator* started publication in March, 1711; and Addison,
though he was drawing £400 a year as Keeper of the Records
in the Bermingham Tower, had some reason to complain of
misfortunes for, as he wrote to Wortley on 21st July, 1711:

I have within this twelvemonth lost a place of £2000 per annum,
an estate in the Indies of £14,000, and what is worse than all the
rest, my mistress. Hear this, and wonder at my philosophy. I find
they are going to take away my Irish place [the keepership] from me
too; to which I must add, that I have just resigned my fellowship,
and that stocks sink every day.

So *The Spectator* had to succeed by providing what its readers wanted. Evidence of sales is uncertain; but it seems that they increased from 3,000 by the 10th number to about 4,000 by the 446th number, when the paper tax reduced the circulation by more than half. If, as Addison claimed, each issue was read by twenty readers, there was one reader of *The Spectator* for every four Londoners. That was a prodigious success, a success owing partly to Steele's discriminating study of contemporary journalism, partly to Addison's skill in reflecting the spirit of the age.

When *The Spectator* started publication, Steele had already had two years' experience of journalism in conducting *The Tatler*, a periodical issued in single sheets, which he had launched in April, 1709. Like *The English Lucian* (1698), *The Tatler* presented news from different quarters of the town: thus accounts of gallantry, pleasure, and entertainments, such as a revival of Congreve's *Love for Love* (*Tatler*, 1), were to be found under the heading of White's Chocolate House; poetry and criticism came from Will's Coffee House, still famous as Dryden's favourite resort; learning came from 'The Grecian,' and foreign and domestic news from St. James's Coffee House, while the heading *From my own Apartment* served to introduce what we should now call an editorial. This division of the sheet was not kept for long. In No. 48 Steele followed the lead of his rival, *The Female Tatler*, which had been appearing in the form of a single-sheet essay since July, 1709. Thereafter *The Tatler* was less and less often divided into sections, less news was offered, and the periodical essay as a form for comment on men, manners, morals, and books was established. The form allowed ample scope for diversity of treatment. Steele seems to have noticed the success Dunton had had in appealing in *The Athenian Mercury* (1691–6) to his readers' taste for moral reform, and in keeping touch with his readers by printing their letters to the editor, either real or imaginary. He had observed how Ned Ward in *The London Spy* (1698–1700) represented contemporary manners by character sketches, and the notion, adopted by Dunton and by Defoe in the early numbers of *The Weekly Review* (1704), of grouping these characters into an imaginary society or club had not escaped his notice. All these devices for attracting readers had been tested in *The Tatler* before being brought to perfection in *The Spectator*.

Addison was in Ireland when the first number of *The Tatler* reached him in May, 1709. He did not know who had written it, but he mentioned in a letter what pleasure it gave to him and to his friends in Dublin. He is believed to have recognized Steele's hand in the fifth number; in the eighteenth his first contribution appeared; and by November he had gained so much ascendancy as to restrain Steele's gossip-mongering proclivities. In *The Tatler* Addison was no more than Steele's highly valued assistant. In *The Spectator* he was Steele's senior partner. He wrote the first number and the tenth, in which *The Spectator's* policy was announced, and he contributed 270 papers to Steele's 240. But though Addison had taken the lead, it was Steele who had taught him his job. Steele had shown him how to use the full range of contemporary journalistic devices and how to insinuate moral reform. Steele had adopted the disguise of a fictitious arbiter of manners and had invented a fictitious club of eccentrics (The Trumpet Club, *Tatler*, 152); and it was Steele who first thought of Sir Roger de Coverley.

Addison's intentions were, broadly speaking, educational. He found in the London of 1711 what Beau Nash found in the Bath of 1705, a society nominally polite but sadly lacking in the decencies of behaviour. Nash's method of reform was to establish a code of etiquette and insist upon its observance. Addison's method was less autocratic. Sometimes *The Spectator* would speak out and denounce an objectionable custom as *The Tatler* had denounced duelling; more often he was content, in Pope's words, to 'hint a fault and hesitate dislike'. Pope was a trifle too harsh when he declared that without sneering Addison 'taught the rest to sneer'; but certainly, without himself laughing, Addison taught others to laugh at ladies who patched their faces in accordance with their political whims or at the absurdities of Italian opera.

Even more delicately oblique is the social criticism conveyed in the De Coverley papers. Steele, who introduced the club members in *Spectator*, 2, seems to have intended them for a group of eccentrics or 'humorists' whose opinions on the way of the world were to be used as texts for the Spectator's comment. But this intention was by no means fully realized. Sir Andrew Freeport, a merchant whose notions of trade were 'noble and generous', is not quoted in *Spectator*, 3, an essay on public trade[1]; nor is the Templar made to voice his opinions on opera in *Spectator*, 5, though he was 'an excellent Critick' and regarded the time of the play as his hour of business. Sir Roger is described by Steele as 'a Gentleman that is very singular in his behaviour, but his singularities proceed from his good sense, and are contradictions to the manners of the world, only as he thinks the world is in the wrong'. This hint was allowed to lie dormant from March till July, when the Spectator paid a visit to Sir Roger's country seat and, during the course of a month's visit, drew the full character of Sir Roger's singularities. The eccentricities of a Tory squire offered ample opportunities for satirical portraiture at the hands of a Whig politician. Addison—the development of Sir Roger's character is mainly Addison's work—did not merely resist this obvious temptation: he made Sir Roger serve his educational purpose in a much more subtle way. Readers were expected to smile at Sir Roger for pronouncing Amen three or four times to the same prayer when pleased with the matter of his devotion, or for rebuking John Matthews in the middle of the service for disturbing the congregation; but it was hoped that the smile would be a smile of affection, and that these oddities of behaviour would make his good qualities the more evident and the more beloved. The lesson of those De Coverley papers which describe Sir Roger's character is a lesson in the extension of human sympathies. The country squire had been an object of ridicule on the Restoration stage, and was still an object of contempt in the City and in fashionable London society. By showing the humanity of the feudal relationship between squire and

[1] Sir Andrew's opinion is quoted in *Spectator*, 69, however, a meditation on the Royal Exchange.

retainer, Addison tried to bring the town into closer sympathy with the country, to substitute affection for ridicule and to convert contempt into respect.

For the purpose of recovering readers out of the desperate state of vice and folly into which the age was fallen, and of encouraging their humanity and common sense, the form of *The Spectator* was nicely adjusted. The daily publication over a space of two years of brief and witty admonitions might be expected to have more effect than the same amount published in volume form. Whether *The Spectator* succeeded in ridding society of certain elements of absurdity and brutality, and in establishing a more decent code of manners, it would be difficult to say. Pope at least thought so, and his evidence is the more striking because he had had reason to complain of Addison's double-dealing. Eighteen years after Addison's death Pope summarized his achievement in a couplet which bears witness to a change in manners:

> He, from the taste obscene reclaims our Youth,
> And sets the Passions on the side of Truth.

But the Spectator's intentions were not only moral. By bringing philosophy out of closets and libraries to dwell in clubs and assemblies, at tea-tables and in coffee-houses, he as well as Berkeley's Alciphron hoped to make Everyman his own philosopher. Addison might have taken his cue from Shaftesbury's *Essay on the Freedom of Wit and Humour*, published two years before the first *Spectator*:

If the best of our modern Conversations are apt to run chiefly upon Trifles; if rational Discourses (especially those of a deeper Speculation) have lost their credit, and are in disgrace because of their *Formality;* there is reason for more allowance in the way of *Humour* and *Gaiety*. An easier Method of treating these Subjects, will make 'em more agreeable and familiar. To dispute about 'em, will be the same as about other Matters. They need not spoil good Company, or take from the Ease or Pleasure of a polite Conversation. And the oftner these Conversations are renew'd, the better will be their Effect. We shall grow better *Reasoners*, by reasoning pleasantly, and at our Ease; taking up, or laying down these Subjects, as we fansy.

Philosophy is brought to the tea-table with all the good humour, gaiety, and ease that Shaftesbury could have wished. A speculation on Temperance is introduced by a story from *The Arabian Nights*, an essay on the attributes of God starts with a description of the scene as 'I was yesterday about sunset walking in the open fields, till the night insensibly fell upon me', and Sir Roger rallies the Spectator on spending so much time among his poultry only to provide an opportunity for discussing the observations of Boyle and Locke on animal instinct. For most of these speculations Addison would have disclaimed any originality since, as he remarks in *Spectator*, 253, 'wit and fine writing doth not consist so much in advancing things that are new, as in giving things that are known an agreeable turn'; and overlooking the claims of the Moderns in scientific discoveries, or perhaps regarding them as plain demonstrations of what was already apprehended,[1] he continues:

It is impossible for us, who live in the latter Ages of the world, to make observations in criticism, morality, or in any art or science, which have not been touched upon by others. We have little else left us, but to represent the common sense of mankind in more strong, more beautiful, or more uncommon lights.

His views were largely derivative, but he could at least claim, what Matthew Arnold in his essay on 'The Literary Influence of Academies' denies him, that he drew upon the best ideas attainable in his time, the ideas not only of the classical philosophers, but of Descartes, Hobbes, and Locke as well; and, as Arnold said in another context, he made those ideas prevail. Dennis complained, with some justification, that Addison had stolen from him without acknowledgment some of the best things in *The Spectator* papers on *Paradise Lost*. It was hard upon Dennis, for he had the more original, penetrating, and energetic mind. But Dennis could not command the Spectator's prestige for persuading the generality of readers that it was 'correct' to admire Milton.

[1]Thus Newton's theory of gravitation seems to have been regarded as a re-expression of Pythagoras's doctrine of attraction. See A. D. McKillop, *The Background of Thomson's Seasons* (Minneapolis, 1942), pp. 31 ff.

In one branch of criticism Addison could claim that he was undertaking something new. The papers on the 'Pleasures of the Imagination' (*Spectator*, 411–421) do, indeed, constitute the first sustained attempt in English to inquire into the principles of beauty in nature and art. Yet even in these papers much of the material is derivative. The doctrine of ideas is borrowed from Locke; and Dennis, who since 1688 had been meditating on the thrilling experience of contemplating the Alps, had awakened an interest in that category of æsthetic experience which became known as The Sublime. To us it is much more rewarding to follow Dennis's pioneering pursuit of The Sublime from his crude definition in *Remarks on Prince Arthur* (1696), to the clearer notion expressed in *The Advancement and Reformation of Poetry* (1701), and thence to the fuller discussion in *The Grounds of Criticism in Poetry* (1704); but we can still admire the way Addison creams Dennis's work and persuades his readers of the 'pleasing astonishment' and 'delightful stillness and amazement in the Soul' which they should experience at the prospect 'of an open champain country, a vast uncultivated desart, of huge heaps of mountains, high rocks and precipices, or a wide expanse of waters'. It was important for appreciation of the poetry soon to be written that readers should recognize what is striking in such experience; it is not the novelty or *beauty* of the sight, but 'that rude kind of magnificence which appears in many of these stupendous works of nature'.

Here and elsewhere Addison confirms the views of more pioneering critics. The debate on the nature of true and false wit had been in progress for some fifty years, when Addison published his papers on Wit (*Spectator*, 58–63), and showed to a generation who still bought new editions of Donne and George Herbert that the Metaphysical manner was not to be admired; and the delights of ballad-collecting and ballad-reading were known to several of the most refined writers of the age before Addison drew his readers' attentions to their charms (*Spectator*, 70, 74).

Addison's criticism of the ballads deserves more than passing attention, for it betrays many of the critical assumptions of the day. They 'have nothing to recommend them', he writes, 'but the beauties of nature', and their 'paintings of Nature' are so inherently simple as to recommend them both to the most ordinary reader and to the most refined. What better evidence could a critic hope to find of the universality of Nature's light, of the direct appeal of Nature to everyone irrespective of age or attainments! Since ballads exhibit the power of Nature in all her simplicity, they must surely obey Nature's laws; and this Addison proceeds to prove by an elaborate comparison of *Chevy Chase* with the *Æneid*. In accordance with the rules of epic poetry, both poets were found to exhibit the same important precept of morality. An epic poet should celebrate persons and actions which do honour to their country: the author of *Chevy Chase* is found to observe the rule as strictly as Homer, Virgil, Statius, and Valerius Flaccus. An epic hero should show generosity of mind: Earl Percy, as he takes the dead Earl Douglas by the hand, 'will put the Reader in mind of *Æneas's* behaviour towards *Lausus*'. And several other passages recall the *Æneid* either in incident or in heroic sentiment. Addison did not infer that the author of *Chevy Chase* 'proposed to himself any imitation of those passages'; the inference he drew was that the poet 'was directed to them in general by the same kind of poetical genius, and by the same copyings after nature'. For Addison *Chevy Chase* seemed to prove the universality of Nature and of those rules that are Nature's laws. Here was a poet ignorant of the rules as critics had codified them, and yet in that dim age Nature's light—that 'clear, unchang'd, and universal light' as Pope characterized it—had shone upon him, and he had thus written as compellingly and truthfully as if he had studied the critics.

Yet Addison constantly admonished his readers not to judge by rule, and his admonishment is in tune with the spirit of the times. The rules, whether as guides to writer or to critic, were felt to have only a limited value. Sir William Temple had said that the utmost that could be achieved by them was 'but to hinder some men from being very ill Poets, but not to make any man a very good one'; the two most successful dramatists of the closing years of the seventeenth century, Congreve and

Vanbrugh, had published their contempt of them; and more recently, Pope echoing Dryden had observed that lucky license could snatch a grace beyond the reach of art. In fact, the countrymen of Shakespeare were eager to allow that there are

> nameless graces which no methods teach,
> And which a master hand alone can reach,[1]

and that these graces were of a nobler order than mechanic beauties achieved by rule. A nobler order, a wilder, more astonishing order, but not necessarily a higher order: this would seem to have been Addison's view. The distinction he draws between such prodigies as Homer, Pindar, and Shakespeare, and the class of genius formed by rule—he instances Plato, Aristotle, Virgil, Cicero, Bacon, and Milton—is a difference of manner rather than of natural ability. In the first group, genius is 'like a rich soil in a happy climate, that produces a whole wilderness of noble plants rising in a thousand beautiful landskips without any order or regularity. In the other it is the same rich soil under the same happy climate, that has been laid out in walls and parterres, and cut into shape and beauty by the skill of the gardener'. To beauties of the first group Addison was undoubtedly sensitive, but he had no technique, or at best an inadequate technique, for expressing his wonder: he is helplessly pleased with the wild solemnity in the speeches of Shakespeare's ghosts, fairies, and witches, but he confesses he has 'no rule by which to judge of them'.

It is such critical asides, as well as such an extended example of 'regular' criticism as the papers on *Paradise Lost*, that show there was still some life in the rules. That Shakespeare was thought to work by some rules of his own seems a legitimate inference from Pope's pregnant remark:

> To judge . . . of *Shakespear* by *Aristotle's* rules, is like trying a man by the Laws of one Country, who acted under those of another.

Pope does not take the further step of discovering what the

---

[1]Cf. *Spectator*, 593: 'Our inimitable *Shakespear* is a stumbling-block to the whole tribe of these rigid Critics. Who would not rather read one of his Plays, where there is not a single rule of the Stage observed, than any production of a modern Critic, where there is not one of them violated?'

rules of Shakespeare's country were; but in that sentence he does at least introduce the principle of relativity into 'regular' criticism, a principle which was to be recognized by the best neo-classical critics of the next generation. Thus when Hurd published his *Letters on Chivalry and Romance* in 1762, he distinguished between the fundamental rules of poetry, such as the universality of its statements, and the rules that are appropriate to particular 'kinds'. For Hurd it is therefore of first importance to recognize the 'kind' before attempting to judge such a work as *The Faerie Queene*. Having distinguished the 'kind', examined other specimens, and investigated the aspect of Nature which the poets of Chivalry and Romance were imitating, Hurd could then deduce the rules which applied in Spenser's country and judge *The Faerie Queene* by those standards. This criticism is written within the neo-classical tradition and shows, perhaps more clearly than the criticism of Addison and Pope, that inherent in the methods of neo-classical criticism was a possibility of growth and development. The tradition was capable of adapting itself to new forms and conditions of writing without changing its essentially 'regular' nature. The rules may change, but the methods by which they were originally found remain unaltered.

CHAPTER IV

SWIFT

To turn from Addison to Swift is to turn from a writer, who
was largely sympathetic towards the aspirations of his fellow
men and felt that their vices and follies were susceptible of
gentle treatment, to one who held a more traditional view of
human depravity. The triumphs of Reason which his contemporaries acclaimed were in Swift's view illusory. Man was indeed
capable of reasoning; but in his fallen state, 'a man's fancy gets
astride of his reason . . . imagination is at cuffs with the senses,
and common understanding, as well as common sense, is
kicked out of doors'.

These words come from *A Tale of a Tub*, written perhaps
in 1696, and published anonymously (as Swift's custom was)
in 1704. In the 'Apology' which he added to the fifth edition
(1710) Swift explains what his purpose had been:

The author was then young [he writes], his invention at the
height, and his reading fresh in his head. By the assistance of some
thinking, and much conversation, he had endeavoured to strip
himself of as many real prejudices as he could; I say real ones,
because, under the notion of prejudices, he knew to what dangerous
heights some men have proceeded. Thus prepared, he thought the
numerous and gross corruptions in Religion and Learning might
furnish matter for a satire, that would be useful and diverting. He
resolved to proceed in a manner that should be altogether new, the
world having been already too long nauseated with endless repetitions
upon every subject. The abuses in Religion, he proposed to set
forth in the Allegory of the Coats, and the three Brothers, which
was to make up the body of the discourse. Those in learning he
chose to introduce by way of digressions.

The corruption in the state of learning was a suitable theme

46

for one who sided with Sir William Temple, the champion of the Ancients in the Battle of the Books. The Ancients' case does not look especially strong to-day, whether we consider the general issue of Ancient superiority in all branches of learning or the particular issue, fought out between Bentley and those wits of Christ Church, Oxford, who upheld the indefensible view that Æsop's *Fables* and the *Letters of Phalaris* are both the oldest and the best books we have. It is so clear to us that the Moderns in the sixteenth and seventeenth centuries had made distinguished advances in the study of physics, astronomy, and medicine, and that Bentley's proof of the inauthenticity of the Phalaris Letters is incontestable, that it is difficult at first to see on what ground the Ancients could make a fight. But the Moderns had overplayed a good hand. Elated by the triumphs of modern scientific discoveries, by the pleasure of correcting venerable and vulgar errors, and more particularly by recognizing that they possessed a new instrument or method of search which promised, in Sir Thomas Browne's words, to complete 'this noble Eluctation of Truth; where, against the tenacity of Prejudice and Prescription, this Century now prevaileth', some members of the Royal Society, notably Sprat and Glanvill, had congratulated the age a little too heartily on the universal light which illuminated the mind of seventeenth-century man, and contrasted so remarkably with the twilight of ignorance covering ancient Greece and Rome. Such intellectual pride deserved rebuke, and Swift administered it:

our noble moderns, whose most edifying volumes I turn indefatigably over night and day, for the improvement of my mind, and the good of my country . . . have, with unwearied pains, made many useful searches into the weak sides of the ancients, and given us a comprehensive list of them. Besides, they have proved beyond contradiction, that the very finest things delivered of old, have been long since invented, and brought to light by much later pens; and that the noblest discoveries those ancients ever made, of art or of nature, have all been produced by the transcending genius of the present age. Which clearly shows, how little merit those ancients can justly pretend to; and takes off that blind admiration paid them by men in a corner, who have the unhappiness of conversing too little with present things.

The easy scorn is more effective than the argument; but it is clear enough that the object of Swift's attack is pride of intellect, and he is relentless in exposing all such empty claims. Just as Peter and Jack in the *Tale* cannot rest content with a plain interpretation of their father's will, but must misuse their intellects to make his will subservient to their desires, so modern man cannot rest content with the plain but arduous route that learning demands. 'We of this age', Swift writes,

have discovered a shorter and more prudent method, to become scholars and wits, without the fatigue of reading or of thinking.

The most accomplished way of using books at present, is two-fold; either, first, to serve them as some men do lords, learn their titles exactly, and then brag of their acquaintance. Or, secondly, which is indeed the choicer, the profounder, and politer method, to get a thorough insight into the index, by which the whole book is governed and turned, like fishes by the tail.

And thus the mountebank scholar is bred. He has plenty to offer if the reader is not too particular:

for what though his head be empty, provided his commonplace book be full, and if you will bate him but the circumstances of method, and style, and grammar, and invention; allow him but the common privileges of transcribing from others, and digressing from himself, as often as he shall see occasion; he will desire no more ingredients towards fitting up a treatise, that shall make a very comely show on a bookseller's shelf.

Such work looks well enough if you are content with a superficial examination; just as a woman looks well enough until she is flayed, and then you would 'hardly believe how much it altered her person for the worse'. This is neither the manner nor the method of the Christian preacher; but it serves the same purpose. It serves to show that 'if it were not for the assistance of artificial mediums, false lights, refracted angles, varnish, and tinsel', the arts which human pride uses to maintain a satisfying illusion, 'there would be a mighty level in the felicity and enjoyments of mortal men'.

Swift wrote this extraordinary book before he had seen much of the world he had already learned to judge so well. It is astonishing that a book which strips the gilding off so much human knavery could have been written by a man whose experience had been limited to life at Trinity College, Dublin, attendance upon Sir William Temple in his retirement at Moor Park, and the duties of an Irish country vicarage.[1] Dr. Johnson, who had no love for Swift, was accustomed to doubt whether *A Tale of a Tub* were his: 'it has so much more thinking', he objected, 'more knowledge, more power, more colour, than any of the works which are indisputably his'.[2] Swift might have sympathized, for many years later he was observed by his cousin, Mrs. Whiteway, looking over the *Tale*, 'when suddenly closing the book, he muttered, in an unconscious soliloquy: "Good God! what a genius I had when I wrote that book!" '[3]

The years ahead were to provide ample material for authenticating his judgments. He came to England in 1707, and again in 1710, as an agent of the Irish bishops to secure the application of Queen Anne's Bounty to the Irish Church. A Whig government had been in power since 1705, enjoying the prestige which Marlborough's victories conveyed; but in 1710 it was clear that it could not survive much longer. Swift was a Whig, as, indeed, a late dependant of Sir William Temple was likely to be. But he was a Whig high-churchman, suspicious of the Whig policy of tolerating dissenters and admitting them to posts of responsibility in affairs of State. The early pages of *The Journal to Stella*, a series of sixty-five letters addressed to his friends Rebecca Dingley and Esther Johnson in Ireland, show both his disgruntlement with the Whigs and his response to the overtures of the Tories, whose church policy he found more acceptable. 'At ten I went to the Coffee-house, hoping to find Lord Radnor, whom I had not seen', he writes to Stella, on 9th September, 1710, the month in which the Whig government fell:

[1]Swift had attended upon William III in 1693 to present Temple's views on the Triennial Bill to the king. Deane Swift tells us that this 'was the first time that Mr. Swift had any converse with courts . . . he told his friends it was the first incident that helped to cure him of vanity'.

[2]Boswell, *Journal of a Tour to the Hebrides*, 16th August.

[3]Scott, *Life of Swift*, 1834, p. 77.

He was there; for an hour and a half we talked treason heartily against the Whigs, their baseness and ingratitude. And I am come home rolling resentments in my mind, and framing schemes of revenge,

and again at the end of the month (30th September):

'Tis good to see what a lamentable confession the Whigs all make me of my ill usage: but I mind them not. I am already represented to Harley as a discontented person, that was used ill for not being Whig enough; and I hope for good usage from him. The Tories dryly tell me, I may make my fortune, if I please; but I do not understand them, or rather, I do understand them.

His lot was thrown in with the Tories, who proceeded to use him as a pamphleteer. At the beginning of November, 1710, he was given the conduct of a weekly paper, called *The Examiner*, which was used to reconcile the country to Tory policy. This paper may be regarded as a political counterpart of *The Spectator;* it amounted, that is to say, to a series of brief pamphlets appearing once a week. So successful were these pamphlets in discrediting the Duke of Marlborough and Whig policy in Church and State, that Swift became one of the most influential men in the Tory party and lived on terms of equality with Harley and Bolingbroke, the party's leaders.

The rise to power had been abnormally rapid and was attended, as such elevations are, by envy and slander. Swift himself has described his experiences in a poem ('The Author upon Himself') written in the summer of 1714, when his political friends were quarrelling and when only a few weeks were to elapse before Queen Anne's death and the eclipse of all Tory hopes for more than a generation:

> S[*wift*] had the Sin of Wit no venial Crime;
> Nay, 'twas affirm'd, he sometimes dealt in Rhime:
> Humour, and Mirth, had Place in all he writ:
> He reconcil'd Divinity and Wit.
> He mov'd, and bow'd, and talk't with too much Grace;
> Nor shew'd the Parson in his Gait or Face;
> Despis'd luxurious Wines, and costly Meat;
> Yet, still was at the Tables of the Great.

Frequented Lords; *saw those that saw the Queen;*
At *Child's* or *Truby's*[1] never once had been;
Where Town and Country Vicars flock in Tribes,
Secur'd by Numbers from the Lay-men's Gibes;
And deal in Vices of the graver Sort,
Tobacco, Censure, Coffee, Pride, and Port.

BUT, after sage Monitions from his Friends,
His Talents to employ for nobler Ends;
To better Judgments willing to submit,
He turns to Pol[it]icks his dang'rous Wit.

AND now, the publick Int'rest to support,
By *Harley* S[wift] invited comes to Court.
In Favour grows with Ministers of State;
Admitted private, when Superiors wait:
And, *Harley*, not asham'd his Choice to own,
Takes him to *Windsor* in his Coach, alone.
At *Windsor* S[wift] no sooner can appear,
But *St. John*[2] comes and whispers in his Ear;
The Waiters stand in Ranks; the Yeomen cry,
Make Room; as if a Duke were passing by.

Now *Finch*[3] alarms the Lords; he hears for certain,
This dang'rous Priest is got behind the Curtain:
Finch, fam'd for tedious Elocution, proves
That S[wift] oils many a Spring which *Harley* moves.
W[alpole] and *Ayslaby*, to clear the Doubt,
Inform the Commons, that the Secret's out:
"A *certain* Doctor is observ'd of late,
"To haunt a *certain* Minister of State:
"From whence, with half an Eye we may discover,
"The Peace is made, and *Perkin* must come over.
York is from *Lambeth* sent, to shew the Queen
A dang'rous Treatise writ against the Spleen;
Which by the Style, the Matter, and the Drift,
'Tis thought could be the Work of none but S[wift] . . . .

[1] A coffee house and tavern, near St. Paul's Cathedral, much frequented by the Clergy.
[2] Viscount Bolingbroke.
[3] Swift's enemy, the Earl of Nottingham.

The Qu[een] incens'd, his Services forgot,
Leaves him a Victim to the vengeful *Scot;*
Now, through the Realm a Proclamation spread,
To fix a Price on his devoted Head.
While innocent, he scorns ignoble Flight;
His watchful Friends preserve him by a Sleight.[1]

BY *Harley's* Favour once again he shines;
Is now caress't by Candidate Divines;
Who change Opinions with the changing Scene:
Lord! how were they mistaken in the Dean!
Now, *Delawere* again familiar grows;
And, in *S[wif]t's* Ear thrusts half his powder'd Nose.
The *Scottish* Nation, whom he durst offend,
Again apply that *S[wift]* would be their Friend.

BY Faction tir'd, with Grief he waits a while,
His great contending Friends to reconcile.
Performs what Friendship, Justice, Truth require;
What could he more, but decently retire?

A wry account of a not uncommon experience. The 'dang'rous
Treatise' shown to Queen Anne by the Archbishop of York was
almost certainly *A Tale of a Tub*, which Swift believed the
Archbishop had shown to the Queen, representing to her at the
same time that the author was unfit to hold high office in the
English Church. The best that Harley could secure him as a
reward for his services was the Deanery of St. Patrick's, Dublin.
It was a poor reward, for in Swift's eyes it was tantamount to
banishment.

To his place of exile he went; but he was soon recalled as
the only man capable of reconciling the two Tory leaders in
the greatest crisis of their party's history. His powers of
mediation were insufficient, and after watching the progress of
the tragedy—Harley's dismissal, the Queen's death, the Whig

---

[1]Williams, in his standard edition of Swift's *Poems*, explains that the
Scots peers, who had been attacked in Swift's pamphlet, *The Public Spirit
of The Whigs*, took action against the printer and publisher. A reward of
£300 was offered for the discovery of the author; but Swift was shielded
by Harley.

triumph, and the Hanoverian succession—he returned to what he hoped would be the seclusion of his deanery. 'I hope I shall keep my Resolution of never medling with Irish Politicks', he wrote to his intimate friend, Charles Ford, in September, 1714, the month after his return. But in spite of his resolution, circumstances compelled him to act. 'No Cloyster is retired enough to keep Politicks out', he told Ford in December, 1719, 'and I will own they raise my Passions whenever they come in my way'. He was about to emerge from his cloister into a period of activity more fruitful, though less splendid, than the old *Examiner* days.

What had raised Swift's passions was his view of the state of Ireland. He discovered a scene of peculiar desolation in a country 'so favoured by Nature . . . both in Fruitfulness of Soil, and Temperature of Climate'. He observed:

the miserable Dress and Diet, and Dwelling of the People . . . the old Seats of the Nobility and Gentry all in Ruins, and no new ones in their Stead; the Families of Farmers, who pay great Rents, living in Filth and Nastiness upon Butter-milk and Potatoes, without a Shoe or Stocking to their Feet; or a House so convenient as an English Hog-sty, to receive them.[1]

These evils he attributed largely to repressive English legislation, which prevented the Irish from enjoying 'the Privilege of a free Trade in all foreign Countries, which will permit them', and also to the non-residence of landlords and office-holders, whose rents and salaries were spent in England and not in the country which produced them. The remedy he proposed was a greater measure of self-sufficiency. In his *Short View of the State of Ireland*, Swift lists fourteen causes of a kingdom's thriving, of which the last two read as follows:

The thirteenth, is, where the People are not obliged, unless they find it for their own Interest, or Conveniency, to receive any Monies, except of their own Coinage by a publick Mint, after the Manner of all civilized Nations.
The fourteenth, is, a Disposition of the People of a Country, to wear their own Manufactures, and import as few Incitements to

[1] *A Short View of the State of Ireland* (1727).

Luxury, either in Cloaths, Furniture, Food, or Drink, as they possibly can live conveniently without.

Both appeal to the argument of self-sufficiency, and both sh w Swift's skill in turning an occasion to political advantage: indeed, they echo his two most notable interventions in Irish affairs. The short and vehement *Proposal for the Universal Use of Irish Manufacture* (1720) and the series of *Drapier's Letters* (1724), where Swift, in the guise of a Dublin draper, urged the Irish people to refuse the copper halfpence coined by 'one William Wood, Hard.Ware.Man' for circulation in Ireland, are those of Swift's pamphlets which most fully justify his claim that he wrote 'to the Vulgar, more than to the Learned'. The sarcasm of the *Proposal* at the expense of 'that *POOR* Kingdom of England' suffering from Irish impositions, and the unscrupulousness of the financial calculations in the first *Letter* from 'M.B., Drapier' are a trifle too obvious; but it must be allowed that Swift knew his readers. He had no high opinion of their intelligence—'one can promise nothing from such wretches as the Irish people', he told Ford when the first *Letter* was published—and he makes little effort to conceal his scorn. 'If the unthinking Shop-keepers in this Town had not been utterly destitute of common Sense', he writes; or again: 'The Scripture tells us, that *Oppression makes a wise Man mad;* therefore, consequently speaking, the Reason why some Men are not *mad*, is because they are not *wise*. However, it were to be wished, that *Oppression* would, in Time, teach a little *Wisdom* to *Fools*'.

Certainly Swift was no demagogue, if by that term is meant a political leader who flatters the people as he rouses them. Rouse them he did, and gained their affections too. We are told that when a reward of £600 was offered for the anonymous Drapier's name no one informed against him, but that instead the citizens of Dublin quoted with relish from the fourteenth chapter of the first book of Samuel:

And the people said unto Saul, Shall Jonathan die, who hath wrought this great salvation in Israel? God forbid: as the Lord liveth, there shall not one hair of his head fall to the ground; for he hath

wrought with God this day. So the people rescued Jonathan, that
he died not.

This second period of Swift's power was differently based, and
possibly gave him deeper satisfaction than the power he exerted
in the last four years of Queen Anne. 'My popularity', he told
Pope, thirteen years later, 'is wholly confined to the common
people, who are more constant than those we miscall their
betters. I walk the streets, and so do my lower friends, from
whom, and from whom alone, I have a thousand hats and
blessings upon old scores'. We may guess that the 'hats and
blessings' were a tribute of recognition to the sense of justice
and compassion which had moved Swift to act in spite of the
scorn he felt for 'such wretches as the Irish people'. These
motives keep breaking in upon the reader of the Irish
pamphlets. 'The Remedy is wholly in your own Hands', he
writes in the fourth *Drapier Letter*,

and therefore I have digressed a little, in order to refresh and
continue that *Spirit* so seasonably raised amongst you; and to let
you see, that by the Laws of *GOD*, of *NATURE*, of *NATIONS*,
and of your own *COUNTRY*, you *ARE*, and *OUGHT* to be a
FREE PEOPLE, as your Brethren in *England*.

As to his compassion, it would be difficult to decide whether
it is more apparent in the wooden-faced irony of *A Modest
Proposal* (1729):

Some Persons of a desponding Spirit, are in great Concern about
that vast Number of poor People, who are Aged, Diseased or
Maimed; and I have been desired to employ my Thoughts, what
Course may be taken, to ease the Nation of so grievous an Incum-
brance. But, I am not in the least Pain upon that Matter; because
it is very well known, that they are every Day *dying*, and *rotting*, by
Cold, and *Famine*, and *Filth*, and *Vermin*, as fast as can be reasonably
expected,

or in *A Short View of the State of Ireland*, where he speaks
straight out because his heart was 'too heavy to continue this
Irony longer'.

Thus we see that Swift's view of his fellow men was
complex. His experience of courts, he told Pope, was that though
they differ,

in some things they are extremely constant. First, in the trite old
maxim of a minister's never forgiving those he has injured: Secondly,
in the insincerity of those who would be thought the best friends:
Thirdly, in the love of fawning, cringing, and tale-bearing: Fourthly,
in sacrificing those whom we really wish well, to a point of interest
or intrigue: Fifthly, in keeping everything worth taking for those
who can do service or disservice. I could go on to four-and-
twentiethly. . . .

In political life he found that all was vitiated by 'party'; even
his friendship with Addison was affected 'by this damned
business of party', he told Stella, in 1710; 'he cannot bear
seeing me fall in so with this ministry'. But the same journal
provides eloquent testimony to the tender regard in which he
held Addison and other friends in either party.

This affection for individuals continually spoilt his
generalizations, and to his credit he recognized it, as a famous
passage from a letter to Pope shows:

I have ever hated all nations, professions, and communities, and
all my love is towards individuals: for instance, I hate the tribe of
lawyers, but I love Counsellor Such-a-one, and Judge Such-a-one:
so with physicians—I will not speak of my own trade—soldiers,
English, Scotch, French, and the rest. But principally I hate and
detest that animal called man, although I heartily love John, Peter,
Thomas, and so forth;

and Swift goes on to say that 'upon this great foundation of
misanthropy', though not with the furious invective of a
Timon, the whole building of his *Gulliver's Travels* (1726) was
erected. The hatred of 'man' in that book, which summarizes
a lifetime's experience, is evident enough in the contemptuous
treatment of Lilliputian politics and Laputan 'projects', in the
King of Brobdingnag's horrified scorn at Gulliver's revelations
of the state of England, and in the description of the bestial
Yahoos; but the hearty love of 'John, Peter, Thomas, and so
forth' is apparent too. 'Who, with the Figure of a *Man*, can
think with Patience of being devoured alive by a *Rat*'? Swift
asks in the second *Drapier Letter*, a theme he had already
elaborated (in manuscript) in the treatment which the tiny
Lilliputian ministers proposed to mete out to the giant Gulliver.
But the Lilliputians were not all so vindictive: Gulliver had at

least two friends at court who were ready to advise mitigation of his sentence and abet his escape. Similarly, in Brobdingnag, Gulliver found at least one giant, his little nurse Glumdalclitch, to shield him with affectionate solicitude from the tribulations which beset him. In Balnibarbi he was received with much kindness by at least one grandee, and entertained in a most hospitable manner; and when finally ejected from the land of the Houyhnhnms, Gulliver from his canoe 'heard the sorrel nag (who always loved me) crying out, *Hnuy illa nyha maja Yahoo*, Take care of thyself, gentle Yahoo'.

The misanthropy is a qualified misanthropy. Mankind is depraved, certainly; but here and there are individuals who serve to test the generalization. And that perhaps is why, desperate as the tone of *Gulliver's Travels* is, Swift could remark on finishing his voyages 'they are admirable things, and will wonderfully mend the world'. Before the world could be mended, man must learn to recognize his truly depraved state. In tearing off the veil of self-deception Swift succeeds better in the 'Voyage to Brobdingnag' than in the 'Voyage to Lilliput'. It is certainly humiliating to be bound and captured by mannikins six inches high—'who, with the Figure of a *Man*, can think with Patience of being devoured alive by a *Rat*'?— but the indignities which Gulliver suffers in Brobdingnag are much grosser:

at last [the farmer] espied me as I lay on the Ground. He considered a while with the Caution of one who endeavours to lay hold on a small dangerous Animal in such a Manner that it shall not be able either to scratch or to bite him; as I myself have sometimes done with a *Weasel* in *England*. . . .

I apprehended every Moment that he would dash me against the Ground, as we usually do any little hateful Animal which we have a Mind to destroy. . . .

There he called his Wife, and shewed me to her; but she screamed and ran back as Women in *England* do at the Sight of a Toad or a Spider.

And when Gulliver expounds the constitution of his country to the King of Brobdingnag, the caution of the farmer and the terror of his wife are amply justified, for the King cannot but conclude from Gulliver's account that 'the Bulk' of Englishmen are 'the most pernicious Race of little odious Vermin that Nature ever suffered to crawl upon the Surface of the Earth'. In the land of the Houyhnhnms Gulliver's humiliation is severer still, for there he recognizes with horror that he more closely resembles the vilest brutes of the country than the rational inhabitants. A severe cooling draught for human pride; and pride, by which the angels fell, was the most dangerous of the deadly sins.

Gulliver closely resembled the Yahoos, but he was not one of them. The Yahoos do not represent Man as he is, but rather Man as he might be if he fell yet further. Gulliver's distinguishing faculty—and Gulliver is Man's representative—is that he still possesses some rudiments of reason. The possession was dangerous, for, as the Houyhnhnms observed, when added to the natural pravity of the Yahoo it might incite Gulliver to anti-social activities beyond the Yahoo's capacity. Yet in those rudiments lay the hope of Man; regeneration. Swift's thinking was at one in this with other thought of the day. The visible world of Nature was believed to owe its beauty and harmony to its obedience to Rule and Order, and what Rule and Order were in the world of Nature Reason was to Man. Dennis put this well when he remarked in his *Advancement and Reformation of Poetry:*

Whatever God created, he designed it Regular, and [as] the Rest of the Creatures cannot swerve in the least from the Eternal Laws pre-ordained for them, without being fearful or odious to us; so Man, whose Mind is a Law to itself, can never in the least transgress that Law, without lessening his Reason, and debasing his Nature. . . .

Since the effect of the Fall was to debase Man's reason, it follows that Man will become regenerate in so far as he recovers his reason.

The primacy of reason is a cardinal point in Swift's teaching in *Gulliver's Travels.* Just as the Master Houyhnhnm detected 'that, our Institutions of *Government* and *Law* were plainly owing to our gross Defects in *Reason,* and by Consequence, in *Virtue;* because Reason alone is sufficient to govern a *rational*

Creature'; so too the King of Brobdingnag 'confined the Knowledge of governing within very *narrow Bounds;* to common Sense and Reason, to Justice and Lenity, to the speedy Determination of Civil and Criminal Causes; with some other obvious Topicks which are not worth considering'. And on that account the king 'professed both to abominate and despise all *Mystery, Refinement,* and *Intrigue,* either in a Prince or Minister', and the Master Houyhnhnm was at a loss to understand 'what I meant by *Law,* and the Dispensers thereof, according to the present Practice in my own Country: Because he thought, Nature and Reason were sufficient Guides for a reasonable Animal'.

At first sight it seems odd that Reason should be set in opposition to such intellectual notions as Government and Law, but it must be remembered that for the Augustans Reason was equated not with 'the subtle niceties of curious wit', but with the *raison* or common sense which is in all men everywhere and always. Reason accepts the universals and the standards which the wise ancients knew, and which remain evermore unchanged; intellect lives in the Academy of Projectors at Lagado trying to extract sunshine from cucumbers, or in the cavils of the schoolmen helping them, as Bacon said, 'out of no great quantity of matter and infinite agitation of wit [to] spin out unto us those laborious webs of learning which are extant in their books'.

Gulliver's Travels is full of the anti-intellectual prejudices of eighteenth-century thinking expounded in Chapter II. As much as Jack and Martin in *A Tale of a Tub,* Swift enjoys stripping the trimmings from the coat he had inherited so as to lay bare the essential simplicity of its outline. The learning of the Brobdingnagians Gulliver found 'very defective; consisting only in Morality, History, Poetry, and Mathematicks . . . the last of these being wholly applied to what may be useful in Life. . . . And, as to Ideas, Entities, Abstractions and Trans-cendentals, I could never drive the least Conception into their Heads'. The clear eye of reason should see no more difference between Whigs and Tories than between high heels and low heels on shoes, and should detect that the wars of religion which cost so many lives were fought to determine 'whether *Flesh* be *Bread*, or *Bread* be *Flesh:* Whether the Juice of a certain *Berry* be *Blood* or *Wine:* Whether *Whistling* be a Vice or a Virtue: Whether it be better to *kiss a Post*, or throw it into the Fire: What is the best Colour for a *Coat*, whether *Black*, *White*, *Red*, or *Grey*; and whether it should be *long* or *short*, *narrow* or *wide*, *dirty* or *clean*; with many more'. Man is not a rational creature, Swift told Pope; but he admitted that he is *rationis capax* and in that admission lay the hopes of his salvation. Because he is *rationis capax*, Swift did not entirely despair. His *Travels* would wonderfully mend the world.

CHAPTER V

POPE

POPE also found a world to mend, a world with which he, like
Swift, felt himself in many ways to be at odds. Neither by
birth nor by training was he ideally prepared for living in it.
The son of elderly parents, he had a crazy body barely capable
of serving the spirit that inhabited it; and as a Roman Catholic
he lived under the shadow of penal laws which restricted his
education and his political activity. To say that his view of the
world was oblique would be an overstatement, but in consequence of his birth and training he was not a full member of
the society in which he lived and of which he presents a
refracted image in his poetry.

Since at best he was 'the gayest *valetudinaire*', and since
he was as a Roman Catholic 'deny'd all Posts of Profit or of
Trust', he could give an undivided mind to the cultivation of
his art. He served a long apprenticeship. His custom as a
boy, he told his friend Spence, was to read as best he could in
the poetry of Greece, Rome, Italy, France, and England,
translating as he went, or imitating what struck his fancy; and
in his earliest published works he can still be observed serving
his apprenticeship of translation and imitation. Apart from his
versions of Statius, Ovid, and Chaucer, he was busy attempting
a variety of poetical 'kinds' to try where his strength lay. After
his Virgilian *Pastorals* (1709), he followed in the steps of
Boileau (and, of course, of Horace) with a poem (*An Essay on
Criticism*, 1711) about the writing of poetry. Boileau's *Le Lutrin*
and Garth's *Dispensary* (1699) suggested to him the idea of a
mock epic, which he fulfilled in *The Rape of the Lock* (1712).
And with Denham's *Coopers Hill* (1642) in mind, he attempted
a 'local poem'—a 'kind' in which the landscape to be described

recalls historic and other associations—and produced *Windsor Forest* (1713). And *Eloisa to Abelard* and the *Elegy to the Memory of an Unfortunate Lady* are best understood as imitations, though more than mere imitations, of Ovid's *Heroical Epistles* and the elegies of Ovid and Tibullus.

These last two pieces were published in 1717 in the first collected volume of his poems. This beautifully printed book contains some of Pope's best work, the perfect revised version of *The Rape of the Lock*, the famous proverbs of the *Essay on Criticism*, and the exquisitely musical versification of the *Pastorals;* but none the less it is a volume of experiments. Looking back on them in later years, Pope was accustomed to make a distinction between these earlier 'fanciful' poems and his mature work in which he wrote of 'Truth' and moralized his song. The early poems do, indeed, exhibit a riot of rococo fancy. Nature never set forth the earth in so rich tapestry, and Pope delivers a golden for her brazen world. His fancy is at its most luxuriant in the description, in *Windsor Forest*, of Old Father Thames arising from his oozy bed to hail the Peace of Utrecht:

> His tresses dropt with dews, and o'er the stream
> His shining horns diffus'd a golden gleam:
> Grav'd on his urn, appear'd the Moon that guides
> His swelling waters, and alternate tydes;
> The figur'd streams in waves of silver roll'd,
> And on their banks *Augusta* rose in gold.
> Around his throne the sea-born brothers stood,
> That swell with tributary urns his flood.
> First the fam'd authors of his ancient name,
> The winding *Isis* and the fruitful *Tame:*
> The *Kennet* swift, for silver Eels renown'd;
> The *Loddon* slow, with verdant alders crown'd:
> *Cole*, whose clear streams his flow'ry islands lave;
> And chalky *Wey*, that rolls a milky wave:
> The blue, transparent *Vandalis* appears;
> The gulphy *Lee* his sedgy tresses rears:
> And sullen *Mole*, that hides his diving flood;
> And silent *Darent*, stain'd with Danish blood.

> High in the midst, upon his urn reclin'd,
> (His sea-green mantle waving with the wind)
> The God appear'd; he turn'd his azure eyes
> Where *Windsor*-domes and pompous turrets rise;
> Then bow'd and spoke; the winds forgot to roar,
> And the hush'd waves glide softly to the shore.[1]

We may readily suppose that Pope paid specially careful attention to this set piece, for he must have been aware that he was challenging two of the greatest of his predecessors, Spenser and Milton, in river catalogues. And not only that. The passage has behind it the long tradition of the court masque: just so might a Caroline dramatist have introduced the masquers at the climax of his piece. It is an exceptionally elaborate and graceful compliment to the Queen.

But triumphantly as Pope has succeeded here, this was not the type of triumph which it pleased him to repeat. *The Rape of the Lock* foreshadows more of his future successes. His rococo fancy is still actively at work, gilding the brazen world of Hampton Court; but he 'stoops to Truth' more often and shows us the world as it is, where court ladies 'shift the moving Toyshop of their heart' and feel the same susceptibility to a stain upon their honour as to a stain upon a new brocade; where 'Wretches hang that Jury-men may Dine'; and where, with fancy and Ariosto to aid him, he can show what things lost on Earth are treasured in 'the Lunar Sphere':

> There Heroes' Wits are kept in pondrous Vases,
> And Beaus' in *Snuff-boxes* and *Tweezer-Cases*.
> There broken Vows, and Death-bed Alms are found,
> And Lovers' Hearts with Ends of Riband bound;
> The Courtier's Promises, and Sick Man's Pray'rs,
> The Smiles of Harlots, and the Tears of Heirs,
> Cages for Gnats, and Chains to Yolk a Flea;
> Dry'd Butterflies, and Tomes of Casuistry.[2]

In this poem we find Pope's first considered view of the world about him, a view which is largely sympathetic. His criticism reminds us of the exactly contemporary *Spectator*'s; and it is still in the mood of *The Spectator* that he moralizes his song,.

[1] ll. 331-54.
[2] v. 115-22.

'fair-sexing' it as Swift might have said, with an imitation of
Sarpedon's address to Glaucus (*Iliad* XII) added to the fifth
canto in 1717 and placed in the mouth of the 'grave *Clarissa*'.
Her part is to remark the inevitable decay of beauty and to
show that what remains when locks, curled or uncurled, have
turned to grey is 'well our Pow'r to use, And keep good
Humour still whate'er we lose'.

Ten years of translating and editing intervened between
these fanciful poems and the poems of Pope's maturity, and
in the interval his sympathy with the world he lived in had
evaporated. It is difficult to give a satisfying reason for this
evaporation. Something can be attributed to his poor physique,
which coupled with the demands of Homer put a stop to the
pleasures of coffee-house life:

> Luxurious lobster-nights, farewell,
> For sober, studious days![1]

Something can be attributed to the wear and tear of his fight
with the Dunces, and something perhaps to his associations
with Swift and with other statesmen out of place. But be the
cause what it may, from 1728 the scene which Pope surveys is
one of ever-darkening corruption.

He first observed this corruption in the world of letters, and
in the conclusion of *The Dunciad* (1728) prophesied what should
come to pass from what 'is already to be seen, in the writings
of some even of our most adored authors, in Divinity, Philosophy, Physics, Metaphysics, &c.'. Perhaps it is Pope's fault
if readers of *The Dunciad* too often regard that poem as a
collection of old scores paid off with interest. Certainly it was
more than that to Pope, who bids us remember 'what the Dutch
stories somewhere relate, that a great part of their Provinces
was once overflow'd, by a small opening made in one of their
dykes by a single *Water-Rat*'. It is the gradual deterioration of
standards which makes him fear that Light will die before the
uncreating word of Dullness, and that 'at her felt approach,
and might, Art after Art goes out, and all is Night'.

The same deterioration was apparent in other arts too.

[1] *A Farewell to London* (1715), ll. 45-6.

When Father Thames rose from his oozy bed in *Windsor Forest*
he prophesied a new age of architectural splendour:

> Behold! *Augusta's* glitt'ring spires increase,
> And Temples rise, the beauteous works of Peace.
> I see, I see where two fair Cities bend
> Their ample bow, a new *White-hall* ascend![1]

But the prophecy was not fulfilled. Twenty years later Pope
could report that the palace of Whitehall was still a ruin, and
that some of those very 'temples', the new churches of Queen
Anne's reign, 'were ready to fall, being founded in boggy
land . . . [and] others were vilely executed, thro' fraudulent
cabals between undertakers, officers, etc.'; while instead of
finding achievements to commend, he was to indite the lavish
cost and little skill expended in building a Timon's villa.
There was ample money for building, and good guidance was
to be had, but:

> Something there is more needful than Expense
> And something previous ev'n to Taste—'tis Sense;[2]

and the Good Sense of Building and Planting he proceeds to
expound[3] in a passage which contains one of the earliest formu-
lations of the principles of landscape gardening.

From the misuse of money by those who could only show
their want of taste, Pope proceeded to a more general survey
of the standards of the moneyed classes in a series of *Ethic
Epistles*, of which the *Epistle to Lord Burlington* already
mentioned was the first to be published. The work was never
completed, but we possess what was to have been the first
book, a survey of the field of study entitled *An Essay on Man*
in four epistles, as well as four more verse essays on the
Characters of Men and Women and on the Use of Riches, a
group usually known as the *Moral Essays*.

Pope was not a systematic thinker. The scraps of Platonism,
Deism, Optimism, Positivism, and Epicureanism which he
tried to piece together into a system still provoke contemptuous

[1] ll. 377–80.
[2] *Moral Essay*, iv, 41–2.
[3] *Epistle to Lord Burlington*, ll. 47 ff.

mirth from professional philosophers. But even the philosophers allow the value of his moral intuitions while they mock his attempts to systematize them. Of these intuitions the most important is the cult of non-attachment. Try to cultivate a serenity of mind—the 'good humour' which 'grave *Clarissa*' had prescribed—for that will make you impervious to the buffets of fortune: don't found your happiness on your intellectual parts, on what your rank in society brings, on the beneficence of your administration as a statesman: don't rely for happiness on the prospect of fame: above all, don't rely on money; yet if you have money, learn this at least, to use it wisely. That was Pope's advice, and his readers had heard it many times before; but it was characteristic of those days that no man resented being told the same thing again and again, so long as it was true and so long as it was said with fresh conviction. Indeed, the older and the more familiar the doctrine the better, for if a doctrine had been tested by one generation after another that successive testing seemed to assure its universal validity. Addison, reviewing Pope's *Essay on Criticism* in *The Spectator* (253), had expressed this view with more conviction than a 'Modern' would have allowed when he represented the impossibility of making observations untouched upon by others: 'We have little else left us, but to represent the common sense of mankind in more strong, more beautiful, or more uncommon lights'. In representing this common sense in uncommon lights, Pope did not content himself with maxims, though his maxims have passed into the proverbial heritage of the language. He illustrates. He shows what is meant by non-attachment or by contentment with a modest competence, and he draws his illustrations from his own life or from the lives of his friends.

It is characteristic of Pope that he rarely saw the good without also seeing the bad in conflict with it. The strong antipathy of good to bad was, as he explained in the *Epilogue to the Satires*, the very provocation of his satire. And so it pleased him to represent two conflicting sets of values: on the one hand, the old Roman simplicity of that secluded villa where he lived at Twickenham; on the other, the luxury and deceitfulness of life at Court and in the City; or (in more individual terms) the philanthropy of 'modest Allen', who 'did good by stealth, and blushed to find it Fame', and on the other hand the colossal frauds perpetrated on the widow and the poor by Blunt of the South Sea Company and Bond of the Charitable Corporation.

To a modern reader such a contrast is purely moral. To a reader of the seventeen-thirties the moral issue was only part of the contrast: the political relevance was equally clear, for since the triumph of the Whigs at Queen Anne's death the party division was less a division between Whig and Tory than between Court and City in alliance against the Country; and Pope was serving his friends who led the opposition to Walpole's government by representing with all his power the contrast of moral values underlying the political conflict.

Experience showed him that poems in imitation of Horace's epistles and satires were more effective for this purpose than further instalments of the *Ethic Epistles*. In this new series of poems (1733–8), the words of Horace are translated and applied to modern conditions, and thus the weight of Roman satiric tradition is enlisted in the fight against modern corruption. In no poem is this moral yet political contrast between two sets of values so clearly represented as in the *Imitation of the First Epistle of the First Book of Horace*, addressed to Bolingbroke, the unofficial leader of the Opposition. Following Horace, Pope produces modern parallels to show that:

> No bugbear is so great,
> As want of figure, and a small Estate.[1]

'Get Mony, Mony still! And then let Virtue follow, if she will' is the doctrine by which all ranks of society seem to govern their lives; and when no higher principle is seen to actuate Court and Government, what can be expected of the rest?

> Their Country's wealth our mightier Misers drain,
> Or cross, to plunder Provinces, the Main:
> The rest, some farm the Poor-box, some the Pews;
> Some keep Assemblies, and wou'd keep the Stews;

[1] ll. 67–8.

Some with fat Bucks on childless Dotards fawn;
Some win rich Widows by their Chine and Brawn;
While with the silent growth of ten per Cent,
In Dirt and darkness hundreds stink content.[1]

The improper regard for money Pope sees alike in the City, where the new Whig financiers were gaining control of trusts and charities, in the Army, at Court, and in Parliament where, as Walpole himself declared, 'all those men have their price'. Pope may have been glancing at this widespread political subservience to the man who paid best when he wrote his epigram for the collar of the Prince of Wales's dog. Certainly it epitomizes the parliamentary situation:

I am his Highness's dog at Kew:
Pray tell me, Sir, whose Dog are you?

To remedy the situation Pope could use his satire to 'brand the bold Front of shameless, guilty Men', and he could hold up for imitation some better standard. The exposure of vice raised the question of the ethics of personal satire, upon which Pope had always placed more reliance than Addison and Swift. The problem had confronted him more than once, but he had no doubt that it was better to single out a few individuals .from the crowd than to deal with the vicious in gross. 'General satire in times of general vice', he told his friend Arbuthnot, 'has no force and is no punishment: people have ceased to be ashamed of it when so many are joined with them . . .', and so he hunted one or two notorious public figures from the herd to represent various manifestations of luxury and corruption. There was Dennis Bond, expelled from the House of Commons in 1732 for breach of trust and convicted of embezzling the funds of the Charitable Corporation shortly after, yet so little discredited that in 1735 he was appointed a churchwarden of St. George's, Hanover Square. There was Francis Chartres, a debauchee who amassed a fortune by gambling and corruption; Gilbert Heathcote, Governor of the Bank of England and the richest commoner in the country, who was, nevertheless, so mean as to dispute the cost of his brother's burial fee; and

[1] ll. 126–33.

John Ward, Member of Parliament for Hackney, convicted
of fraud and forgery, who amused himself during his term of
imprisonment by giving poison to cats and dogs to see them
expire by slower or quicker torments. The list could be
extended with minor court officials and small office-holders as
well as with pseudonymous characters of uncertain identity,
such as Timon the tasteless Magnifico, and Sir Balaam the
City Knight, who came to a bad end through speculation and
accepting bribes from the French. But the list is representative.
Though not one was an eminent politician, the political
allegiance of each was to Walpole's party, and thus each example
served to emphasize that it was such men as these who prospered
under Walpole's administration, and that the administration
was favourable to the spread of corruption in all walks of life.
Once more Pope is tempted to prophecy, this time in less
exalted strain:

> At length Corruption, like a gen'ral flood
> (So long by watchful Ministers withstood)
> Shall deluge all; and Av'rice, creeping on,
> Spread like a low-born mist, and blot the Sun;
> Statesman and Patriot ply alike the stocks,
> Peeress and Butler share alike the Box,
> And Judges job, and Bishops bite the town,
> And mighty Dukes pack Cards for half a crown.
> See Britain sunk in lucre's sordid charms,
> And France reveng'd of *ANNE*'s and *EDWARD*'s arms.[1]

But the picture was not wholly black. The very fact of contrast,
of that strong antipathy of good to bad, suggests that in Sodom
and Gomorrah there are still some righteous men left; and they
are to be found (of course) amongst the ranks of the Parliamentary Opposition. In his brief characters of these men, Pope
builds up his standard of political and moral probity. Have we
been sickened by ministerial equivocation? Then let us observe
the leader of the Jacobite Tories:

> I love to pour out all myself, as plain
> As downright *Shippen*, or as old *Montagne:*[2]

[1] *Moral Essay*, iii, 135–44.
[2] *Imit. Hor. Sat. II. i*, ll. 51–2.

Have we been disgusted by too many examples of meanness and depravity? Then:

> Would ye be blest? despise low Joys, low Gains;
> Disdain whatever *CORNBURY* disdains;
> Be Virtuous, and be happy for your pains.[1]

Does the spirit of patriotism seem dead? We need only look at one of Walpole's young opponents:

> Sometimes a Patriot, active in debate,
> Mix with the World, and battle for the State,
> Free as young Lyttelton, her cause pursue,
> Still true to Virtue, and as warm as true;[2]

or at one of the older Opposition Whigs:

> And you! brave *COBHAM*, to the latest breath
> Shall feel your ruling passion strong in death:
> Such in those moments as in all the past,
> 'Oh, save my Country, Heav'n!' shall be your last.[3]

Are there no examples of non-attachment in this world of greedy and grasping politicians? Certainly there are, and they could often be found in Pope's grotto at Twickenham:

> Where, nobly-pensive, *ST JOHN* sate and thought;
> Where *British* sighs from dying *WYNDHAM* stole,
> And the bright flame was shot thro' *MARCHMONT*'s Soul.
> Let such, such only tread this sacred Floor,
> Who dare to love their Country, and be poor.[4]

In his letters to Pope, Swift more than once expresses his concern about the durability of Pope's poetry. So much of it dealt with 'town facts and passages' that a man living in Dublin found it obscure and feared he must be losing abundance of the satire. Pope must presumably have been aware of the risk; but if he gave it much thought he must have reflected that good verse has embalming qualities. If the creatures whom Pope lampoons were well chosen as representative types we shall

[1]*Imit. Hor. Ep. I. vi*, ll. 60–2.
[2]*Imit. Hor. Ep. I. i*, ll. 27–30.
[3]*Moral Essay*, i, 262–5.
[4]*On his Grotto at Twickenham*.

recognize them well enough however little we know about their
personal history. Who Paridel was everyone has forgotten, but
we recognize him as soon as we meet him in *The Dunciad:*

> Thee too, my Paridel! she mark'd thee there,
> Stretch'd on the rack of a too easy chair,
> And heard thy everlasting yawn confess
> The Pains and Penalties of Idleness.[1]

Of Lord Harvey's character, on the other hand, a man can
discover as much as he wants to know; yet he is not likely to
inquire unless he has first responded to Pope's description of
'this Bug with gilded wings, This painted Child of Dirt that
stinks and stings'. It is the forcibleness and variety of the
imagery employed to penetrate into the essence of character
which compels our admiration and preserves Pope's satiric
poetry; for its object (as Wordsworth wrote of very different
poetry) 'is truth, not individual and local, but general, and
operative; not standing upon external testimony, but carried
alive into the heart by passion; truth which is its own
testimony. . . .'

Furthermore, the reader's response is assisted by the diction
and verse in which this imagery is conveyed. Coleridge remarked
that in one of his lectures he had had occasion to point out 'the
almost faultless position and choice of words' in Pope's satires
and moral essays. So far as choice is concerned, Pope might
have said with Wordsworth that the language of his later poetry
was 'a selection of the language really spoken by men'. The
dictions proper to mock-heroic ('the glitt'ring *Forfex*' for
'scissors'), to pastoral ('rural dainties', 'swelling clusters'), and
to elegy ('polish'd marble', 'kind domestic tear') are unsuited
to moral and satiric poetry. There Pope may be said to talk
with distinction; but the talk is varied, and ranges from the
easy colloquy of much of the first *Imitation*, or the irritation
of the first lines of the *Epistle to Dr. Arbuthnot*, or the rapid
repartee with which the *Epilogue to the Satires*, II, opens to the
rapt, enthusiastic tones with which it closes. And the flow of
the verse changes with the mood of the talk. Just as the blank

[1] iv, 341–4.

verse of Shakespeare and Milton grows more and more supple
at the end of their careers, so too Pope plots more and more
startling variations on the standard rhythms of the couplet.
Only long practice could achieve such a contrapuntal triumph
as

> Shut, shut the door, good *John!* fatigu'd I said,
> Tye up the knocker, say I'm sick, I'm dead,[1]

or as this passage of dialogue:

> 'Ye Rev'rend Atheists!'—'Scandal! name them, Who?'—
> 'Why that's the thing you bid me not to do.'[2]

As a young man Pope had expressed some fear of monosyllabic
lines: 'unless very artfully managed', he told Cromwell, 'they
are stiff, languishing, and hard'. Yet what could be more rapid
than the last line quoted, which should be scored musically
with an *accelerando* and *crescendo* leading to a *sforzando* on the
eighth syllable. A languishing line may be used appropriately
too, witness the long drawn-out expression of contempt which
the monosyllables give in:

> Pretty! in Amber to observe the forms
> Of hairs, or straws, or dirt, or grubs, or worms.[3]

And position, as Coleridge remarked, is most important also.
Pope frequently relies on the emphasis which the caesura can
give to the preceding or succeeding stress to underline an
ironic word or a significantly chosen image. Such additional
emphasis is given to the italicized word in the following
examples:

> A hundred footsteps *scrape* the marble Hall . . .[4]
> And sit *attentive* to his own applause . . .[5]
> Bear the mean Heart that *lurks* beneath a Star.[6]

Such is Pope's workmanship within the limits of the couplet.

[1]*Ep. to Arbuthnot*, ll. 1–2.
[2]*Epilogue to the Satires*, ii, 18–19.
[3]*Ep. to Arbuthnot*, ll. 169–70.
[4]*Moral Essay*, iv. 152.
[5]*Ep. to Arbuthnot*, l. 210.
[6]*Imit. Hor. Sat. II. i*, l. 108.

This detailed care should not lead us to assume that each couplet is a unit wholly distinct from its fellows. From his earliest days Pope had paid attention to the organization of the verse paragraph. This is evident from a letter to Cromwell, written in 1710, where Pope observes that the same rhymes should not be repeated within four or six lines of each other, and that the natural pauses at the fourth, fifth, or sixth syllables should not be continued above three lines together, without the interposition of another. He may be watched observing his rule in *The Rape of the Lock* or *The Dunciad*. In each poem there are couplets or pairs of couplets which appear to have been modelled independently of their context. A good example is the parody of Denham's description of the Thames in *Coopers Hill*, at the expense of a minor poet:

> Flow Welsted, flow! like thine inspirer, Beer,
> Tho' stale, not ripe; tho' thin, yet never clear;
> So sweetly mawkish, and so smoothly dull;
> Heady, not strong; o'erflowing, tho' not full.[1]

Such lines could live separately as an epigram, and doubtless Pope contrived to find a final resting-place in *The Dunciad* for his epigrams, just as he used his *Epistle to Dr. Arbuthnot* for collecting odds and ends of verse written from time to time. Nevertheless *The Dunciad* is as remarkable for the grandeur of its extended passages as for its wit and the beauty of its imagery. The noble conclusion, celebrating the final triumph of Dulness, has often been admired. Scarcely less splendid is the burlesque in Book III (27 ff.) of that passage in *Æneid VI* where Æneas is guided by the Sibyl to the infernal regions. The effect is exceedingly complicated because so many different levels of response are involved. The passage is built out of contemporary detail. Dunce after dunce is slaughtered to provide the 'raptur'd Monarch's' vision, so that the reader might complain of the transitoriness of the satire if it were not for the amber preserving these grubs and worms. When Pope wrote of his enemies' poetry:

[5]*Dunciad*, iii, 168–72.

> Some strain in rhyme; the Muses, on the racks,
> Scream like the winding of ten thousand jacks,[1]

he was dealing with the source of his irritation as the oyster
is said to deal with its disease. He made it into pearl. The
passage is encrusted with pearl of this kind; but that is not all
that the reader is compelled to admire. He enjoys the ludicrous
effect of the parody of Virgil; yet as he reaches the climax he
doubts whether this is burlesque, whether the pomp is not
genuine after all. The roll-call of proper names has been
borrowed from Milton to assist the parody of epic. But when
Pope declaims:

> Lo! where Mæotis sleeps, and hardly flows
> The freezing Tanais thro' a waste of snows,
> The North by myriads pours her mighty sons,
> Great nurse of Goths, of Alans, and of Huns![2]

he can scarcely be convicted of travesty, though presumably a
burlesque was his initial intention. 'You hardly know whether
to laugh or weep', wrote Hazlitt of the apotheosis of foppery
and folly in *The Rape of the Lock*. The same doubt attends
the reader of *The Dunciad*. It is built out of the ugly, the
trivial, and the commonplace, and yet Pope has achieved the
sublime.

[1] *Dunciad, iii*, ll. 159–60
[2] ibid., ll. 87–90.

CHAPTER VI

THOMSON

WORDSWORTH'S praise of Thomson has accustomed us to think of him as a man born out of time, a man who alone amongst his fellows could fix his eye steadily upon an object and whose feelings could urge him 'to work upon it in the spirit of genuine imagination'. He was certainly a gifted poet, but not an unaccountable phenomenon. The time was ripe for a long, meditative poem on the beauties of nature, and *The Seasons*[1] was wholeheartedly accepted by contemporary readers.

The mood in which Thomson approached his task had been admirably conveyed by Addison in *Spectator*, No. 393. Reflecting as he so often did upon the duty of cheerfulness, Addison remarks that

> The Creation is a perpetual feast to the mind of a good man, every thing he sees chears and delights him; Providence has imprinted so many smiles on Nature, that it is impossible for a mind, which is not sunk in more gross and sensual delights, to take a survey of them without several secret sensations of pleasure. . . .
> Natural Philosophy [he continues] quickens this taste of the Creation, and renders it not only pleasing to the imagination, but to the understanding. It does not rest in the murmur of brooks, and the melody of birds, in the shade of groves and woods, or in the embroidery of fields and meadows, but considers the several ends of Providence which are served by them, and the wonders of divine Wisdom which appear in them. It heightens the pleasures

---

[1] *Winter* was first published in 1726, two years before *The Dunciad*. *Summer* and *Spring* followed in 1727 and 1728, and *Autumn* appeared for the first time in the first collected edition of *The Seasons* in 1730. Thomson corrected and enlarged the four poems from time to time. Quotations in this and other chapters are taken from J. Logie Robertson's edition (Oxford, 1908).

of the eye, and raises such a rational admiration in the Soul as is little inferior to devotion;

and Addison concludes his paper with the recommendation 'to moralize this natural pleasure of the Soul', and graft upon it a religious exercise of praise and thanksgiving. The importance of this passage is not merely that it recognizes the delight every man feels at the coming of spring or at the full display of summer, but that it both rationalizes and moralizes that delight.

Rationalization had been made possible by Sir Isaac Newton, whose work seemed to confirm that most ancient and cherished belief in an orderly disposed universe. Earlier philosophers had apprehended the divine mechanics of the universe; Newton was felt to have produced demonstrable truth. What had hitherto been darkly apprehended was now clearly seen. Pope, in fact, was expressing the view of the educated layman when he wrote for Newton's epitaph:

> Nature and Nature's Laws lay hid in night.
> God said, 'Let Newton be', and all was Light.

The immediate connexion between Newton's work and the contemplation both of the beauty of Nature and of Nature's Creator was emphasized by Roger Cotes, the Plumian Professor of Astronomy at Cambridge, in a preface he wrote for the second edition of Newton's *Principia* (1713):

The gates are now set open, and by this means we may freely enter into the knowledge of the hidden secrets and wonders of natural things. He has so clearly laid open and set before our eyes the most beautiful frame of the System of the World, that, if King *Alphonsus* were now alive, he would not complain for want of the graces either of simplicity or of harmony in it. Therefore we may now more clearly behold the beauties of Nature, and entertain ourselves with the delightful contemplation; and, which is the best and most valuable fruit of philosophy, be thence incited the more profoundly to reverence and adore the great *MAKER* and *LORD* of all.

Thanks to Newton, Man could now contemplate the harmony underlying the beauties of Nature and could reverence the divine handiwork with a keener sense of wonder and rapture.

The poet's task in this new dispensation was clear. Newton had given him something to sing about. He had heightened the pleasures of the poet's eye and had raised 'such a rational admiration in [his] Soul' as was 'little inferior to devotion'. That Thomson recognized this is clear from his account of the rainbow. Not for him to wonder idly at its beauty on a spring evening; his rapture is heightened by what Newton had told him:

> Meantime, refracted from yon eastern cloud,
> Bestriding earth, the grand etherial bow
> Shoots up immense, and every hue unfolds,
> In fair proportion running from the red
> To where the violet fades into the sky.
> Here, awful Newton, the dissolving clouds
> Form, fronting on the sun, thy showery prism;
> And to the sage-instructed eye unfold
> The various twine of light, by thee disclosed
> From the white mingling blaze.[1]

When a comet appears the superstitious and the guilty tremble; but 'the enlightened few',

> Whose godlike minds philosophy exalts,
> The glorious stranger hail. They feel a joy
> Divinely great; they in their power exult,
> That wondrous force of thought, which mounting spurns
> This dusky spot, and measures all the sky.[2]

Thus it comes about that, 'tutored' by Philosophy (Newtonian Physics, that is),

> Poetry exalts
> Her voice to ages; and informs the page
> With music, image, sentiment, and thought,
> Never to die; the treasure of mankind,
> Their highest honour, and their truest joy![3]

The poet's task is complementary to the natural philosopher's. While the natural philosopher propounds a hypothesis to

[1] *Spring*, ll. 203–12.
[2] *Summer*, ll. 1715–19.
[3] ibid., ll. 1753–7.

account for the appearance and behaviour of things, the poet
presents the synthesis he sees in the natural philosopher's work,
and voices that sense of wonder with which 'the sage-instructed
eye' beholds the course of Nature now so satisfactorily
explained. Thomson's way of expressing this relationship is
to say that the natural philosopher traces

> from the dreary void,
> The chain of causes and effects to Him,
> The world-producing Essence, who alone
> Possesses being;

while the poet receives

> The whole magnificence of heaven and earth,
> And every beauty, delicate or bold,
> Obvious or more remote, with livelier sense,
> Diffusive painted on the rapid mind.[1]

If the poet is to enter into partnership with the Newtonian
physicist, it behoves him to be accurate in his observation and
therefore to keep his eye steadily fixed upon his object. To this
we owe the precise description of the auriculas in *Spring*
'enriched With shining meal o'er all their velvet leaves' and of
the robin's behaviour in *Winter*, as well as many a 'georgic'
detail derived, as Mr. McKillop has shown,[2] from Bradley's
General Treatise of Husbandry and Gardening. But though the
relationship with natural philosophy demands accuracy of
description—and it is no less loving description for being
accurate—the poet must never forget his proper character. His
mind has been 'exalted' by natural philosophy; he feels 'a joy
divinely great', and it is within his power to raise in his readers
'such a rational admiration as is little inferior to devotion'.
Thomson is almost too conscious of the rapture demanded of
him. The mood is constantly invoked either by comment or by
the exaltation conveyed in the act of describing. This is the
unifying principle underlying the heterogeneous material of
The Seasons. That this was Thomson's aim seems clear from

[1] *Summer*, ll. 1745–52.
[2] *The Background of Thomson's Seasons* (Minneapolis, 1942), pp. 45 ff.

the advice he gave to his friend Mallet, who was attempting the same type of poetry at about the same time:

My idea of your poem is a description of the grand works of Nature raised and animated by moral and sublime reflections: therefore before you quit this earth you ought to leave no great scene unvisited. Eruptions, earthquakes, the sea wrought into a horrible tempest, the abyss amidst whose amazing prospects, how pleasing must that be of a deep valley, covered with all the tender profusion of the spring. Here if you could insert a sketch of the deluge, what more affecting and noble? Sublimity must be the characteristic of your piece.

The advice shows that Thomson appreciated the distinction between the Sublime and the Beautiful thirty years before Burke published his *Inquiry* (1756). That need cause no surprise; for though no writer before Burke had attempted such a clear-cut distinction as he, the contrast between the Sublime and the Beautiful had been hinted by Addison in those *Spectator* papers on the Pleasures of the Imagination where he mentions the 'delightful stillness and amazement in the Soul' felt in contemplating the more stupendous works of nature. It was but a step for Thomson to recognize that the poetry which describes such things arouses 'rapturous terror'.

One section of Burke's *Inquiry* which we may suppose that his contemporaries appreciated is his classification of ideas that are sublime. Terror he regarded as the ruling principle, since it robs the mind of reasoning and hurries us on by an irresistible force. 'Serpents and poisonous animals' raise ideas of the sublime because they are considered as objects of terror; so does obscurity which prevents us from realizing the nature of danger; and so do greatness of dimension and ideas of eternity and infinity which lie beyond our reason. Power is 'a capital source of the sublime' especially if it be uncontrollable, as in a thunder storm, or representative of destructive strength like the bull. All 'general privations', such as vacuity, darkness, solitude, and silence, are great because they are terrible. 'Magnificence is likewise a source of the sublime'; and so are various effects of light, such as lightning and that light 'which by its very excess is converted into a species of darkness'.

Later critics might object that Burke had confused practical and æsthetic emotions. Thus Payne Knight pointed out that the figure of Burke walking down St. James's Street without his breeches and with a loaded blunderbuss in his hand would be an object of terror and astonishment, but could not be called sublime. Yet we should recognize, none the less, that Burke had been honestly attempting to decide how he had been affected and not how he ought to have been affected, what experiences were accompanied by the 'sublime' thrill and not what should accompany it. Whether reading Thomson had helped Burke in his categorization we do not know, but it is surprising how many items in his list can be observed in Thomson's diploma pieces. Let us imagine a lover of Thomson's poetry re-reading *Summer* after studying Burke's *Inquiry*. Is it not highly probable that he would attribute the sublimity of the following description to the ideas of uncontrollable and destructive power, the greatness of dimensions, the blinding flashes of light illuminating obscurity, which unite in conveying the effect of terror?

> 'Tis listening fear and dumb amazement all:
> When to the startled eye the sudden glance
> Appears far south, eruptive through the cloud,
> And, following slower, in explosion vast
> The thunder raises his tremendous voice.
> At first, heard solemn o'er the verge of heaven,
> The tempest growls; but as it nearer comes,
> And rolls its awful burden on the wind,
> The lightnings flash a larger curve, and more
> The noise astounds, till overhead a sheet
> Of livid flame discloses wide, then shuts
> And opens wider, shuts and opens still
> Expansive, wrapping ether in a blaze.
> Follows the loosened aggravated roar,
> Enlarging, deepening, mingling, peal on peal
> Crushed horrible, convulsing heaven and earth.
>
> Down comes a deluge of sonorous hail,
> Or prone-descending rain. Wide-rent, the clouds
> Pour a whole flood; and yet, its flame unquenched,
> The unconquerable lightning struggles through,

Ragged and fierce, or in red whirling balls,
And fires the mountains with redoubled rage.
Black from the stroke above, the smouldering pine
Stands a sad shattered trunk; and, stretched below,
A lifeless group the blasted cattle lie:
Here the soft flocks, with that same harmless look
They wore alive, and ruminating still
In fancy's eye; and there the frowning bull,
And ox half-raised. Struck on the castled cliff,
The venerable tower and spiry fane
Resign their aged pride. The gloomy woods
Start at the flash, and from their deep recess
Wide-flaming out, their trembling inmates shake.
Amid Carnarvon's mountains rages loud
The repercussive roar: with mighty crush,
Into the flashing deep, from the rude rocks
Of Penmenmaur heaped hideous to the sky,
Tumble the smitten cliffs; and Snowdon's peak,
Dissolving, instant yields his wintry load.
Far seen, the heights of heathy Cheviot blaze,
And Thulė bellows through her utmost isles.[1]

No doubt our imaginary reader would have been pleased by
the tender contrast of innocent love which follows, describing
the fate of Amelia caught in the storm and struck by lightning
from the embrace of Young Celadon, and by the concluding
lines of description in which the sublime of the storm gives way[2]
and

> a glittering robe of joy,
> Set off abundant by the yellow ray,
> Invests the fields, yet dropping from distress.
> 'Tis beauty all . . .

In his section on the sublimity of obscurity Burke had
noticed 'how greatly night adds to our dread, in all cases of

---

[1] *Summer*, ll. 1128–68.

[2] Professor Tillotson notes (ed. *The Rape of the Lock and other poems*, 1940, p. 310 *n*) that 'the sudden oasis—"beauty lying in the lap of horror"— had been strongly presented in *Paradise Lost*, iv, 131 ff., and was to endear itself to all eighteenth-century æstheticians'.

danger, and how much the notion of ghosts and goblins, of which none can form clear ideas, affect minds, which give credit to the popular tales concerning such sorts of beings'. Thomson had noticed this, too. He especially commends his friend Mallet's 'shrieking witches in the desert—at the dead of night', and the lovers in his own poem wandering at night shun

> The lonely tower . . . whose mournful chambers hold,
> So night-struck-fancy dreams, the yelling ghost,[1]

while in the storms of winter,

> they say, through all the burdened air
> Long groans are heard, shrill sounds, and distant sighs,
> That, uttered by the demon of the night,
> Warn the devoted wretch of woe and death.[2]

Thomson's references to country superstitions are few and fragmentary, and are introduced with a note of amused disbelief befitting his role of philosopher and disciple of Sir Isaac Newton. But it is remarkable that they are found at all. Aubrey records the disappearance of the last fairy in the year 1670, not far from Cirencester: 'being demanded, whether a good spirit or a bad? returned no answer, but disappeared with a curious perfume and most melodious twang'. It was time he went, for the spirit of the age was unfavourable to his survival. Sprat, who blames the poets for imposing 'the Deceit', remarks in his *History of the Royal Society* that

from the time in which the *real Philosophy* has appear'd, there is scarce any whisper remaining of such *Horrors:* Every Man is unshaken at those Tales at which his *Ancestors* trembled: The course of Things goes quietly along in its own true Channel of *Natural Causes* and *Effects*. For this we are beholden to *Experiments;* which though they have not yet compleated the Discovery of the true World, yet they have already vanquish'd those wild Inhabitants of the false Worlds, that us'd to astonish the Minds of Men;

[1]*Summer*, ll. 1679–81.
[2]*Winter*, ll. 191–4.

and Hobbes remarks parenthetically in *Leviathan* that 'the *Fairies* have no existence, but in the Fancies of ignorant people, rising from the Traditions of old Wives, or old Poets'. What could a poet do, forced to breathe this emancipated air? He could scarcely admit unquestioning belief; but to anyone who objected the improbability, he could boldly adopt Dryden's defence of the epic poet and say that he

is not tied to a bare representation of what is true, or exceeding probable; but that he may let himself loose to visionary objects, and to the representation of such things as depending not on sense, and therefore not to be comprehended by knowledge, may give him a freer scope for imagination. 'Tis enough that, in all ages and religions, the greatest part of mankind have believed the power of magic, and that there are spirits or spectres which have appeared. This, I say, is foundation enough for poetry.[1]

Addison held the same opinion. He too breathed emancipated air; but he was not pleased at 'seeing through the falsehood' and willingly gave himself up to 'so agreeable an imposture'. The poet, he thought, might 'fall in with our natural prejudices, and humour those notions which we have imbibed in our infancy'; such descriptions, he felt, might 'raise a pleasing kind of horrour in the mind of the Reader, and amuse his imagination with the strangeness and novelty of the persons who are represented in them'.[2] The descriptions, in fact, might prove an agreeable source of the sublime.

This was Thomson's justification, and the justification of Blair and Collins, of Gray in his 'Welsh' and 'Norse' poetry, and of Macpherson in his *Ossian*, poets who instinctively felt that disbelief was more willingly suspended in favour of the traditional beliefs of the more remote, less cultivated fringes of these islands. They recognized what contemporary critics insisted, that suspension of disbelief was encouraged by the power of association. They did not need Alison to tell them, for example, that

[1] *Of Heroic Plays, an Essay.*
[2] *Spectator* 419.

the hooting of the Owl at midnight, or amid ruins, is strikingly Sublime. The same Sound at noon, or during the day, is trifling or ludicrous. The scream of the Eagle is simply disagreeable, when the bird is either tamed or confined; it is Sublime only, when it is heard amid Rocks and Deserts, and when it is expressive to us of Liberty, and Independence, and savage Majesty.[1]

Superstitious horrors were known to require for effective treatment an atmosphere of gloom, most readily produced by fierce torrents, forbidding mountains, ravens, moping owls, and ivy-mantled ruins. These became the traditional stage-properties of romanticism. Garth had used several of them in his poem, *Claremont* (1715), where we find 'a Grott . . . with hoary Moss o'ergrown, Rough with rude Shells, and arch'd with mouldring Stone'; and Pope had used many more in *Eloisa to Abelard* (1717), ll. 129–170. But an even larger consignment of the brood of fear had been transported from France by Katherine Philips, some fifty years earlier, in her version of *La Solitude de St. Amant*. In the following verses the notion of pleasing horror is already apparent:

> O how agreeable a sight
> These hanging mountains do appear
> Which the unhappy would invite
> To finish all their sorrows there.

> What beauty is there in the sight
> Of these old ruin'd castle walls
> On which the utmost rage and spight
> Of Time's worst insurrection falls.

> The raven with his dismal cries,
> That mortal augury of Fate,
> Those ghastly goblins gratifies
> Which in these gloomy places wait.

Such was the gloom which gathered round the forsaken lover. He is found in *Spring*, 'with head declined, And love-dejected eyes'.

[1]Archibald Alison, *Essays on the Nature and Principles of Taste* (1790), 3rd ed., 1812, i. 222.

> Sudden he starts,
> Shook from his tender trance, and restless runs
> To glimmering glades and sympathetic glooms,
> Where the dun umbrage o'er the falling stream
> Romantic hangs.[1]

'Romantic': the word was beginning to gain some of the rich associations with which later eighteenth-century use endowed it.

Professor Lovejoy has observed that it would be more proper to speak of romanticisms than Romanticism; and one of Thomson's most engaging qualities for the historian is that he can detect several romanticisms in *The Seasons*. Amongst the most prominent is Thomson's humanitarianism, his sympathy with misery and oppression in all its forms. At first sight it seems paradoxical that such sympathy was widespread at a time when the lowest orders of society were so ruthlessly treated. We have all heard of the horrors of life on board a man-of-war, the tyranny of the press gang, the shocking state of debtors' prisons and lunatic asylums, the iniquities of child labour and the slave trade, the colossal financial swindles, and the deplorable effects of cheap gin. The impression we deduce of a coarse and insensitive age is justifiable; but we should reflect that we derive this impression largely from the satirical work of Pope, Hogarth, Fielding, and Smollett, all of whom were angered by what they saw. Eighteenth-century England was, indeed, full of individuals working to improve the conditions they had inherited. We remember the pioneers in prison reform—Oglethorpe, praised by Pope for his 'strong benevolence of soul', Howard and Elizabeth Fry; but we have forgotten the names of those who were subscribing money for the building of hospitals and for the victims of the Lisbon earthquake in 1755. This widespread sympathy was regarded by contemporaries as one of the most striking characteristics of the age. The Rev. John Brown, whose *Estimate of the Manners and Principles of the Time* (1757) was by no means favourable, was constrained to allow that the 'Lenity of our Laws in capital

[1] *Spring*, ll. 1024–8.

Cases; our Compassion for convicted Criminals; even the general Humanity of our Highwaymen and Robbers' were proofs that 'the Spirit of Humanity is natural to our Nation'; and in the following year Dr. Johnson admitted in *Idler*, No. 4, that though the age was not likely to be remembered as a splendid period of our history, yet 'no sooner is a new species of misery brought to view and a design of relieving it proposed, than every hand is open to contribute something, every tongue is busied in solicitation, and every art of pleasure is employed for a time in the cause of virtue'.

To account for this spirit of universal benevolence is difficult. Something can be attributed to the influential teaching of the Cambridge Platonists, to Richard Cumberland's *Treatise of the Laws of Nature*, and to the recommendations of benevolence in the sermons of Tillotson, Barrow, and Sherlock.[1] But no man proclaimed so confidently as Shaftesbury that virtue consists in promoting the good of others and that a 'taste' or 'moral sense' prompts us to benevolent actions. Thomson had read Shaftesbury's *Characteristics* and had taken to heart his moral teaching: he claims him in *Summer* as one of the most famous of Britannia's worthies:

> The generous Ashley thine, the friend of man,
> Who scanned his nature with a brother's eye,
> His weakness prompt to shade, to raise his aim,
> To touch the finer movements of the mind,
> And with the moral beauty charm the heart.[2]

Without the inspiration of the *Characteristics* it seems unlikely that Thomson would have made such frequent and varied appeals to his readers' humanitarian instincts. Scattered through *The Seasons* are numerous passages expressing sympathy with those who 'pine in want, and dungeon-glooms, Shut from the common air and common use Of their own limbs', with slaves, with over-worked labourers, and with all forms of 'suffering worth lost in obscurity'. If only man would give thought to

[1] A. R. Humphreys, ' "The Friend of Mankind" (1700–60)—An Aspect of Eighteenth-Century Sensibility', *The Review of English Studies*, xxiv (1948), pp. 203 ff.

[2] ll. 1551–5.

'the thousand nameless ills that one incessant struggle render life', then surely, he reflects,

> The conscious heart of Charity would warm,
> And her wide wish Benevolence dilate;
> The social tear would rise, the social sigh;
> And, into clear perfection, gradual bliss,
> Refining still, the social passions work.[1]

Thomson's charity also extended to suffering animals. Pope had already denounced the Englishman's love of blood-sports, and had taught his readers that 'the more entirely the Inferior Creation is submitted to our Power, the more answerable we should seem for our Mismanagement of it';[2] and as the century proceeded more and more writers are found testifying to the hatred of this brand of cruelty. The sight of the stag at bay, which Thomson describes with all the compassion at his command,[3] moved even Somervile to pity, though his theme in *The Chase* (1735) was the praise, pursuit, and justification of English hunting:

> Beneath a weight of woe he groans distress'd,
> The tears run trickling down his hairy cheeks:
> He weeps, nor weeps in vain. The king beholds
> His wretched plight, and tenderness innate
> Moves his great soul. Soon at his high command
> Rebuk'd, the disappointed hungry pack
> Retire submiss, and, grumbling, quit their prey.[4]

Indeed, as Dr. de Levie remarks,[5] 'Nothing points more clearly to the increase of hostile criticism of hunting than the numerous vindications of this sport on the part of the lovers of the hunt'. Even more striking is the sympathy expressed for the caged bird. The sight was to put 'all Heaven in a rage' by the end of the century; but long before Blake's outburst,

---

[1] *Winter*, ll. 354-8.
[2] *Guardian*, No. 61 (1713).
[3] *Autumn*, 449-57.
[4] iii, 593-9.
[5] D. de Levie, *The Modern Idea of the Prevention of Cruelty to Animals and Its Reflection in English Poetry* (1947), p. 77.

Thomson's muse had bemoaned 'her brothers of the grove' inhumanly caught by 'tyrant man',

> and in the narrow cage
> From liberty confined, and boundless air;[1]

and forty years later, Sterne was to vow that he had never had his affections more tenderly awakened than by a starling fluttering about in a little cage and crying: 'I can't get out—I can't get out'. For the Man of Feeling the caged bird had become a symbol of Liberty unnaturally confined, and so clearly was this recognized that Master Blifil had no difficulty in justifying his malicious action of releasing Sophia Western's pet. "Indeed, uncle", he said to Mr. Allworthy, "I am very sorry for what I have done. . . . I had Miss Sophia's bird in my hand, and thinking the poor creature languished for liberty, I own I could not forbear giving it what it desired; for I always thought there was something very cruel in confining anything".[2] We should expect this explanation to appeal to Square, whom Fielding represents as a disciple of Shaftesbury; but even Allworthy, sorry as he felt at Sophia's disappointment, was impressed by Master Blifil's 'generous motive'.

But let us return for a moment to Thomson's sigh for suffering worth lost in obscurity. That sigh was to be echoed by many a poet, for worth lost in obscurity, whether suffering or not, was to become one of their favourite themes. The still sad music of humanity is to be heard before 1720 in Parnell's 'Night Piece on Death', when the poet meditates on

> Those Graves, with bending Osier bound
> That nameless heave the crumbled Ground,
> Quick to the glancing Thought disclose
> Where *Toil* and *Poverty* repose.
>   The flat smooth Stones that bear a Name,
> The Chissels slender help to Fame. . .
> A middle Race of Mortals own,
> Men, half ambitious, all unknown:

[1] *Spring*, ll. 701–5.
[2] Fielding, *Tom Jones* (1749), Bk. IV, ch. 3.

and the same music is heard again in the more lasting expression
which Gray gave to the theme, when meditating on the pathos
of those mute, inglorious Miltons lying in a country churchyard:

> Chill Penury repress'd their noble rage,
> And froze the genial current of their soul.

In this connexion it is worth recalling that Queen Caroline
patronized a Wiltshire labourer called Stephen Duck, who had
described in halting verse the pitiless rigour of an agricultural
labourer's life, that Shenstone as early as 1737 could consider a
village schoolmistress a fit subject for a poem of three hundred
lines, that Dr. Johnson wrote his most moving verses on the
death of an obscure, uncouth, slum-doctor, a very lowly
profession in the eighteenth century, and that (in Carlyle's
words) 'A Scottish peasant's life was the meanest and rudest
of all lives, till Burns became a poet in it, and a poet of it; found
it a *man's* life, and therefore significant to men'. When Burns
exclaimed:

> What tho' on hamely fare we dine,
>   Wear hodden-gray, and a' that?
> Gie fools their silks, and knaves their wine,
>   A man's a man for a' that,

he was saying more emphatically, as his custom was, what many
of his contemporaries had learned to think.[1]

The years lay ahead when a leech-gatherer could be divined
as something more than man, when a shepherd on the fells
could be seen as

> A solitary object and sublime,
> Above all height! like an aerial Cross,
> Stationed alone upon a spiry Rock
> Of the Chartreuse, for worship,[2]

---

[1] It is not only Gray and Burns who insist upon the equality and fraternity
of men underlying social distinctions. Richardson also remarks upon it in a
notable passage in his novel *Pamela* (1740, Everyman edition, i. 234). And
all three are indignant at the disdainfulness of the men of high degree
towards their humbler brethren. If there had been a political revolution in
England at the end of the eighteenth century, critics to-day might be detecting
in these writers what Lytton Strachey heard in Beaumarchais' *Le Mariage
de Figaro*—'far off, but distinct—the flash and snap of the guillotine'.

[2] Wordsworth, *The Prelude*, viii, 272-5.

and when the epitaph of a country girl was to be:

> Rolled round in earth's diurnal course,
> With rocks, and stones, and trees.

In those lines of Wordsworth we all recognize one of the many notes of romanticism, but from what has already been said it is clear that this romanticism was not unprepared for. What Thomson called 'the Power of Philosophic Melancholy' had long been infusing tenderness through the breast of many a Man of Feeling, awakening 'a throb for virtue', and arousing 'the love of nature unconfined, and, chief, Of human race'.

CHAPTER VII

IMITATION, AND ORIGINAL COMPOSITION —THOMSON, COLLINS, AND SHENSTONE

WE are sometimes asked to believe that Pope, like Donne before him,

> rul'd as hee thought fit
> The universal Monarchy of Wit;

but at no stage of his life were the critics unanimous about his standing as a poet. Though we must make some allowance for the personal animosity of the Dunces who attacked his work, and even of such an acute critic as Dennis, no such allowance need be made for the doubts expressed about his poetry after his death. 'Pope he was inclined to degrade from a poet to a versifier', Johnson wrote of Dick Minim, a character in *The Idler* (1759) who retails the critical cant of the day; and if this represents the taste of the time it is not surprising that Pope had few imitators among the major poets of the next generation. Cowper remarked in *Table Talk* (1782) that 'ev'ry warbler had his tune by heart'; but where are they? Churchill[1] in the seventeen-sixties and Gifford in the seventeen-nineties learned something from him in satire, and Cowper himself modelled the poems of his first published volume upon the colloquial manner of Pope's verse epistles. But no one could mistake their workmanship for Pope's; and the other masters of the couplet, Johnson, Goldsmith, and Crabbe, wrote in a quite distinctive manner. If one poet exercised a wider influence upon eighteenth-century poetry than another that poet was Milton.

The reasons for Milton's reputation amongst the Augustans

---

[1]Churchill professed to have formed himself on the model of Dryden, but in *The Farewell* at least he strongly reminds us of Pope's later satire.

are not far to seek. As early as 1688 Dryden had equated him with Homer for surpassing 'loftiness of thought' and with Virgil for 'majesty'; and although poets were no longer quite so anxious to excel in epic poetry, the epic still retained its prestige as the chosen form of the greatest of the ancients. Thus Milton was revered as the best of our epic poets. Secondly, he was considered the greatest exponent of the Sublime. Thirdly, it was not difficult to make his achievements accord with neo-classical theories of poetry; for was he not a poet of 'General Nature', a writer dealing in great and universal truths, truths (as Johnson said) 'habitually interwoven with the whole texture of life' and a moral (as Addison said) 'the most universal and most useful that can be imagined'; and did not his example show that the way to imitate Nature was to imitate the ancients? It is not surprising, therefore, that his poetry was copied in a mechanical way, that his diction became one of the sources of eighteenth-century poetic diction, and that his blank verse, his octosyllabics, and even the stanza of the Nativity Ode and the irregular verse of *Lycidas* were used as models by eighteenth-century poets.

Miltonic blank verse had been used by several writers[1] before John Philips began burlesquing his 'darling Milton' in 'The Splendid Shilling' (1701) and employing 'Miltonian verse' for more serious purpose in his 'georgic' poem *Cyder* (1708). The lead he gave in choosing blank verse for a 'georgic' was followed after an interval of time by several other writers, notably by Somervile in *The Chace* (1735), Armstrong in *The Art of Preserving Health* (1744), and Dyer in *The Fleece* (1757). The reason for the choice of blank verse is obscure. Perhaps Milton's verse was thought to lend an extraneous dignity to the inescapable vulgarities of a largely attractive theme. What could poor Grainger, the poet of *The Sugar-Cane* (1764), do when called upon to describe the havoc made by mice and rats in a sugar plantation? He might have turned it into a mock-heroic with a parody of Homer's battle of the frogs and mice. This was his original intention, for which blank verse would

---

[1] R. D. Havens in *The Influence of Milton on English Poetry* (1922) has noticed about 150 pieces in blank verse between *Paradise Lost* and *Winter*.

have been well enough suited. But he feared (so Boswell tells us) that the introduction of rats, in a grave poem, might be liable to banter, so he had recourse to a periphrasis:

> Nor with less waste the whisker'd vermin race
> A countless clan despoil the lowland cane.

Even to such a ludicrous evasion of the difficulty as this a casual inspection of Milton's verse would lend some colour. Thus an 'imitation' of Milton suited Grainger's purpose whatever he did. In the same way it suited Dyer's purpose when he felt that an epic simile or a roll-call of proper names would serve to ennoble his picture of industrial England:

> Such was the scene
> Of hurrying Carthage, when the Trojan chief
> First viewed her growing turrets. So appear
> Th' increasing walls of busy Manchester,
> Sheffield, and Birmingham, whose reddening fields
> Rise and enlarge their suburbs.[1]

The reason for Thomson's choice of blank verse is less difficult to discover. Blank verse would make an obvious appeal to a poet with such strong dislike for limitations of every kind. Furthermore, Shaftesbury had commended Milton for throwing off 'the horrid Discord of jingling Rhyme';[2] and that from a man whose teaching he so much admired might have been sufficient reason in itself even if Milton had not been recognized as the greatest exponent of the sublime. Since sublimity was to be the characteristic of Thomson's work, it would have been thought perverse not to follow Milton. We have already observed his Miltonic imitation of the 'sudden oasis of beauty lying in the lap of horror'; and he can also be observed studying Milton's inversions ('our strengthen'd bodies in its cold embrace Constringent'), his adverbial use of the adjective ('with fruit empurpled deep'), his compound epithets ('dim-discover'd', 'dusky-mantled'), his periphrases and his latinisms.

But we should take care not to regard Thomson as Milton's sedulous ape. Thomson's latinisms came naturally to a lowland

[1] *The Fleece*, iii, 335–40.
[2] 'Advice to an Author' (1710), II, i.

Scot writing Southern English, and his periphrases were used
not to escape vulgarity, but precisely and evocatively.[1] It was
not the meanness of the word 'egg' that he wished to avoid
when describing the young birds in *Spring* breaking 'their
brittle bondage'. The periphrasis enabled him to draw attention
to the single attribute of the egg required by the context. Nor
did he aim at the grandeur of generality in referring to birds
as 'the fearful race', for 'fearful' is the most apt generic term
to describe both the 'white-winged plover' when she

> wheels
> Her sounding flight, and then directly on
> In long excursion skims the level lawn

to tempt 'the unfeeling schoolboy' from her nest, and the
heath-hen fluttering 'o'er the trackless waste . . . to lead The
hot pursuing spaniel far astray'. Thomson needed these
periphrases and must have found them even if Milton had
never written, though Milton's example provided him with
encouraging authority. Nor did Thomson write of 'The
infuriate hill that shoots the pillared flame' when he meant
'volcano', as some critics have assumed. The periphrasis and
the noun are not equivalent. The periphrasis serves not only
to evoke the 'sublime' thrill; it so controls and directs the
reader's associations that he shares that thrill. The mere noun
is incapable of either. The mere noun leaves the reader's
associations free and undirected. At the word 'fish' the reader
is at liberty to think of Billingsgate, bad language and bad smells,
but 'finny prey' ensures that his attention is fixed upon the
creature caught by an angler.

No one can possibly ignore the Miltonic echoes in
eighteenth-century blank verse, and Mr. Eliot has, indeed,
suggested that these echoes were inescapable. It is the more
remarkable that some poets should have avoided them. Thus
Thomson, for all that the groundwork of his verse is Miltonic,
achieves a more breathless and excited rhythm in some of his

[1]The subject of eighteenth-century diction is examined in three important
essays by Professor Geoffrey Tillotson in his *Augustan Studies* (London,
1961).

'sublime' passages. We notice some Miltonic devices in the following description of a river in spate, but the rhythmical pattern is nothing like Milton's, it is more like Pope's:[1]

> Resistless, roaring, dreadful, down it comes,
> From the rude mountain and the mossy wild,
> Tumbling through rocks abrupt, and sounding far;
> Then o'er the sanded valley floating spreads,
> Calm, sluggish, silent; till again, constrained
> Between two meeting hills, it bursts a way
> Where rocks and woods o'erhang the turbid stream;
> There, gathering triple force, rapid and deep,
> It boils, and wheels, and foams, and thunders through.[2]

Similarly the Miltonic rhythms of Somervile's *Chace* give way to a more broken staccato verse at the excitement of a check in the hunt:

> See how they toss, with animated rage
> Recov'ring all they lost!—That eager haste
> Some doubling wile foreshews. —Ah! yet once more
> They're check'd—Hold back with speed—On either hand
> They flourish round—ev'n yet persist—'Tis right;
> Away they spring; the rustling stubbles bend
> Beneath the driving storm.[3]

But more remarkable was Young's achievement in *Night Thoughts* (1742–7). There is more of *Tamburlaine* (or perhaps of Pistol) than of Milton in

> Death! Great proprietor of all! 'tis thine
> To tread out empire, and to quench the stars;[4]

and though there are plenty of Miltonic imitations in Young's verse, the groundwork is exclamatory and epigrammatic. He had observed that Pope did not need the full scope of the couplet for turning such epigrams as 'A little learning is a

---

[1]Compare the passage from Pope's *Iliad* (xxiii, 144 f.) quoted by Professor Tillotson in his *On the Poetry of Pope* (Oxford, 1938), p. 44.

[2]*Winter*, ll. 97–105.

[3]*The Chace*, ll. 252–8.

[4]*Night Thoughts*, i. 205–6.

dang'rous thing' or 'Hope springs eternal in the human breast'.
The limits of the blank verse line were enough. What Young
showed, in such a passage as this, was that blank verse could
be broken down to units even more terse and sententious than
the couplet contained:

> Throw years away?
> Throw empires, and be blameless. Moments seize;
> Heaven's on their wing: A moment we may wish,
> When worlds want wealth to buy. Bid day stand still,
> Bid him drive back his car, and reimpose
> The period past, regive the given hour.
> Lorenzo, more than miracles we want;
> Lorenzo—O for yesterdays to come![1]

So generally acceptable was this Senecan abruptness that
Joseph Warton was led to propose a new punctuation for the
first line of Gray's *Elegy:*

> The curfew tolls! The knell of parting day!

It was not only Milton's blank verse that eighteenth-century
poets imitated. The octosyllabics of *L'Allegro* and *Il Penseroso*
were used by Parnell for his 'Hymn to Contentment' (1714)
and his 'Night Piece on Death', and by Dyer when he aban-
doned the Pindaric stanzas in which he had first written
'Grongar Hill' (1726); and many of the elegies written from
1740 onwards are described by their authors as imitations of
Lycidas.

But none of these poets was so discriminating a Miltonian
as Collins. He and his friend Joseph Warton had meditated
collaboration in a volume of odes which was evidently intended
to be a *Lyrical Ballads* of experiment and reform. The project
came to nothing—perhaps because there was so much over-
lapping in subject[2]—and the odes were published in separate
volumes, Warton's in 1746 and Collins's in 1747.

[1] *Night Thoughts*, ii. 305-12.

[2] Or perhaps, as Professor Woodhouse suggests (*Studies in English by
Members of University College, Toronto*, 1931, p. 92 *n*), because Dodsley
the publisher accepted Warton's poems but appears to have refused those
of Collins.

The principal value of Warton's *Odes* is that they help us to understand Collins's poetic purpose. In his preface Warton writes:

The public has been so accustomed to didactic poetry alone, and essays on moral subjects, that any work where the imagination is much indulged, will perhaps not be relished or regarded. The author, therefore, of these pieces is in some pain, lest certain austere critics should think them too fanciful or descriptive. But he is convinced that the fashion of moralising in verse has been carried too far, and as he looks upon invention and imagination to be the chief faculties of a poet, so he will be happy if the following Odes may be looked upon as an attempt to bring back poetry into its right channel.

The inference is that Warton was proposing a revolt from the manner of Pope's later poetry and that reform was to be promoted by establishing the primacy of the imagination. But what did Warton mean by 'imagination'? The term is evidently equivalent with 'fancy' and 'description', and that deduction from the preface is borne out by the poems themselves, which are filled with the generalized imagery of *L'Allegro* and *Il Penseroso*. Warton has selected certain images, lying well within every man's experience, to embody his abstractions. Thus:

> AUTUMN cooling caverns seeks
> And stains with wine his jolly cheeks,

and:

> WINTER, like poor pilgrim old,
> Shakes his silver beard with cold;

and the nature of Fancy is implied as much by a description of her dwelling as by a portrait of the nymph herself:

> O lover of the desart, hail!
> Say, in what deep and pathless vale,
> Or on what hoary mountain's side,
> 'Mid fall of waters you reside,
> 'Mid broken rocks, a rugged scene,
> With green and grassy dales between,[1]
> 'Mid forest dark of aged oak,
> Ne'er echoing with the woodman's stroke,

[1] One more 'sudden oasis—"beauty lying in the lap of horror" '.

> Where never human art appear'd,
> Nor ev'n one straw-roof'd cott was rear'd,
> Where NATURE seems to sit alone,
> Majestic on a craggy throne.

Collins's interest, like Warton's, lay in descriptive poetry, as the title of his volume indicates, *Odes on Several Descriptive and Allegoric Subjects;* and he also exercised his image-making faculty to embody his abstractions. But whereas Warton aimed at a L'Allegro-like distinctness of image, Collins attempted a carefully meditated lack of definition. Thus Collins conveys the mood of evening, not as Warton does with a succession of distinct and generalized pictures:

> To the deep wood the clamorous rooks repair,
> Light skims the swallow o'er the wat'ry scene,
> And from the sheep-cotes, and fresh-furrow'd field,
> Stout ploughmen meet to wrestle on the green—

but with Corot-like indistinctness:

> Or if chill blustring Winds, or driving Rain,
> Prevent my willing Feet, be mine the Hut,
> That from the Mountain's Side,
> Views Wilds, and swelling Floods,
> And Hamlets brown, and dim-discover'd Spires,
> And hears their simple Bell, and mark o'er all
> Thy Dewy Fingers draw
> The gradual dusky Veil.

Like Warton, Collins implies the nature of his abstractions in his descriptions of their haunts; but whereas Warton's Fancy lives in a commonplace 'cell' with woodbine round the door and a hawthorn above it, Collins's Poetical Character dwells

> High on some Cliff, to Heav'n up-pil'd,
> Of rude access, of Prospect wild,
> Where, tangled round the jealous Steep,
> Strange shades o'erbrow the Valleys deep,
> And holy *Genii* guard the Rock,
> Its Gloomes embrown, its Springs unlock;

his Fear is to be found

>   in haunted Cell,
> Where gloomy *Rape* and *Murder* dwell;
> Or, in some hollow'd Seat,
> 'Gainst which the big Waves beat,
> Hear drowning Sea-men's Cries in Tempests brought!

and his Danger

>   stalks his Round, an hideous Form,
>   Howling amidst the Midnight Storm,
>   Or throws him on the ridgy Steep
>   Of some loose hanging Rock to sleep.

Collins, as Dr. Johnson remarked, was indeed 'eminently delighted with those flights of imagination which pass the bounds of nature', and nowhere is this delight more evident than in the posthumous 'Ode on the Popular Superstitions of the Highlands of Scotland', written about the year 1749. Little more than twenty years had elapsed since Thomson had cautiously introduced these superstitions into *The Seasons* with an air of amused disbelief; but a change in taste and feeling permitted Collins to 'hold each strange Tale devoutly true', and bid the muse sustain 'the rural faith':

>   These are the themes of simple, sure effect,
>   That add new conquests to her boundless reign,
>   And fill, with double force, her heart-commanding strain.

Dr. Johnson doubted the command which strains such as these could exercise upon the heart. 'This idea which [Collins] had formed of excellence led him to oriental fictions [Johnson had the *Persian Eclogues* (1742) in mind] and allegorical imagery, and perhaps, while he was intent upon description, he did not sufficiently cultivate sentiment'. Not sufficiently perhaps; yet he did cultivate it, for not only is the episode of the drowned crofter ('Popular Superstitions' Ode, st. viii) informed with human feelings, but Collins frequently uses these aerial beings as agents of sympathy with the fate of men, most notably in the 'Ode Written in the beginning of the Year 1746'. No human figure, however generalized, is there called to lament 'the Brave, who sink to Rest, By all their Country's Wishes

blest'. Collins provides an allegorical figure—Spring—to deck
their graves and, as usual, represents the nature of his
abstraction by calling attention to one significant part, her
'dewy Fingers cold'; and, characteristically, the knell is rung
by 'Fairy Hands' and the dirge sung by 'Forms unseen'. All
is depersonalized—though not dehumanized—to the utmost
degree, as comparison with the 'Ode to a Lady on the Death of
Colonel Ross', apparently an earlier treatment of the same
theme, will show. Yet the '1746' Ode is a most moving lament
and the most finished product of Collins's imagination. He has
presented certain ideas by means of allegorical symbols and
has exercised his image-making faculty not merely in describing
those symbols, but in 'flights of imagination which pass the
bounds of nature'.

What has Collins drawn from his study of Milton? Little
enough by comparison with what is original in his poetry. In
the first place, we may notice that though he finds no occasion
for Miltonic blank verse, he sees that other Miltonic verse
forms are well suited to his purpose. The 'Nativity Ode'
stanza is adapted for the 'Ode to Simplicity', the octosyllabics
of 'L'Allegro' and 'Il Penseroso' are used for the antistrophes
of the 'Ode to Fear' and the 'Ode on the Poetical Character',
and most distinctive of all, the unrhymed stanza which Milton
used for translating Horace's 'Ode to Pyrrha' helps Collins to
convey that deliberate lack of definition which characterizes
the 'Ode to Evening'. But more important than this is the
origin of Collins's, as of Warton's, imaginative poetry in their
study of Milton. Warton we have seen was content with little
more than mimicry of L'Allegro, but Collins with more
originality of mind used his study of Milton's imagery as a
point of departure for much more ambitious work.

Though no other poet exercised so wide an influence as
Milton, Spenser also had his admirers and imitators. The
admiration he excited shows how ready eighteenth-century
readers were to enjoy poetry diametrically different from what
was being written at the time, and poetry which made severe
demands both upon the understanding and upon neo-classic
standards of taste. But the Spenser they admired was not

Wordsworth's 'Sweet Spenser, moving through his clouded heaven With the moon's beauty and the moon's soft pace'; he was a poet of 'a warm and boundless Fancy' certainly, a poet whose 'Embellishments of Description are rich and lavish . . . beyond Comparison', and a poet who clothed his moral teaching in allegorical garb, but above all he was a poet who treated rustic and even gross subjects with engagingly childlike innocence. It was this aspect of Spenser's work which Pope as a boy tried to imitate in 'The Alley'. The grossness of that poem has not suited the taste of later times, but Pope's contemporaries thought that he had succeeded admirably in representing what they called Spenser's 'ludicrous' or sportive manner. 'When I bought Spenser first', wrote Shenstone to his friend Richard Graves in 1742,

I read a page or two of the Fairy Queen, and cared not to proceed. After that, Pope's Alley made me consider him ludicrously; and in that light, I think, one may read him with pleasure. I am now . . . from trifling and laughing at him, really in love with him. I think even the metre pretty (though I shall never use it in earnest); and that the last Alexandrine has an extreme majesty.

At the time he wrote that letter Shenstone had just finished preparing a revised edition of his poem 'The Schoolmistress' which had first been published in 1737, and was to be revised once more in 1748. In this idyll of a village dame-school Shenstone was attempting to imitate Spenser's 'language, his simplicity, his manner of description, and a peculiar tenderness of sentiment, remarkable throughout his works'. The 'tenderness of sentiment' was well suited to the spirit of the age. Here for the first time we find that affectionate yet condescending treatment of village life which was to be more notably expressed in Goldsmith's Deserted Village (1770) and George Morland's genre paintings (c. 1780–90). Shenstone dwells lovingly upon the dame's cap 'far whiter than the driven snow, Emblem right meet of decency . . .', her apron 'dy'd in grain, as blue, I trowe, As is the hare-bell that adorns the field', her russet stole and kirtle, and her elbow chair. With Spenser as his authority for noticing such trivial detail, Shenstone could devote a whole stanza to

One ancient hen she took delight to feed,
The plodding pattern of the busy dame;
Which, ever and anon, impell'd by need,
Into her school, begirt with chickens, came;
Such favour did her past deportment claim:
And if neglect had lavish'd on the ground
Fragment of bread, she would collect the same;
For well she knew, and quaintly could expound,
What sin it were to waste the smallest crumb she found;

and as many as eight stanzas—(seven too many)—describe the
dame using her birch rod on an urchin whose little sister stood
by watching the punishment in helpless agony of mind. Bewick
could have managed it better in one of his tail-pieces, just as
Gray, in his 'Ode on a Distant Prospect of Eton College', was
to improve upon Shenstone's picture of Fate's 'little victims' at
play. The detail and treatment of many a later poem and many
a water-colour and woodcut are here; and oddly enough,
Spenser is responsible for the release of this sentiment, for in his
'quaint' and 'ludicrous' particularity of description Shenstone
found the authority he needed for flouting neo-classic
orthodoxy.

The revisions Shenstone made in his text show a progressive
restraint in his use of Spenser's language. To write 'everich'
where 'every' would have done was a good joke at first, but it
was a joke which palled; and in the later versions Shenstone
seemed to be using obsolete words largely to convey a rustic
and 'ludicrous' effect. Just as there was one diction appropriate
for satire, another for elegy, and another for the 'sublime', so
there was a diction appropriate for the 'ludicrous', at once
'simple' and obsolete. That was Thomson's view as well. In
the 'Advertisement' to *The Castle of Indolence* (1748) he writes:

This Poem being writ in the manner of Spenser, the obsolete words,
and a simplicity of diction in some of the lines which borders on the
ludicrous, were necessary to make the imitation more perfect.

The poem had been started about 1733 as a sportive trifle 'in
the way of raillery on himself, and on some of his friends, who
would reproach him with indolence, while he thought them at
least as indolent as himself'. In spite of this emphasis upon the

'ludicrous', that is not the main impression the reader is left with. He will recognize the 'ludicrous' in stanza LIV of Canto 1 describing the 'puzzling sons of party' who 'whisper[ed] close, now shrugging rear[ed] The important shoulder', but when at last they are 'pushed up to power . . . In comes another set, and kicketh them down stairs', and he will find it again in the last stanza of the poem; but he will see too that Thomson is more concerned to imitate Spenser the allegorist. The first and better of the two Cantos is an eighteenth-century anticipation of 'The Lotos-Eaters', and was evidently inspired by Spenser's description of the Bower of Bliss in the second canto of *The Faerie Queene*. Thomson's Spenser is much closer than Shenstone's Spenser to the romantic dreamer admired by nineteenth-century critics; witness the fiends

> Who hurl the wretch as if to hell outright
> Down, down black gulfs where sullen waters sleep,
> Or hold him clambering all this fearful night
> On beetling cliffs,[1]

or the wood

> Of blackening pines, ay waving to and fro [that]
> Sent forth a sleepy horror through the blood,[2]

or the picture of the 'pleasing land of drowsyhed . . .'

> Of dreams that wave before the half-shut eye;
> And of gay castles in the clouds that pass,
> For ever flushing round a summer sky.[3]

The measure of the difference between Thomson's descriptions in *The Seasons* and in *The Castle of Indolence* is the difference between the sublime and the voluptuous, and it is the new voluptuousness in Thomson's work that Spenser is responsible for releasing. In this poem Thomson no longer needs the pomp of diction, the evocative periphrases of *The Seasons*, he relies now on 'simple' and 'obsolete' words not

[1] I, xlvi.
[2] I, v.
[3] I, vi.

merely for 'ludicrous' but for voluptuous effect. The verbal debt to Spenser which he and other Spenserians were prepared to admit is acknowledged in footnotes or in the glossaries they appended to their poems and which they largely borrowed from the glossary to Hughes's edition of Spenser (1715). In these glossaries we expect to find such evidence of playfulness as 'Certes, *certainly*', 'Hight, *is called*', 'Whilom, *ere-while*, *formerly*', 'Ycleped, *called, named*'; it is more surprising to find in need of definition such words as the following: 'aghast', 'appal', 'avail', 'carol', 'dreary', 'forlorn', 'glee', 'guerdon', 'miscreant', 'poignant', 'ribauld', 'uncouth', 'welkin'. If the Spenserians had done nothing else they would deserve recognition for restoring to the poetic vocabulary words like these which carry an aura of romance about them. But Thomson and his fellow Spenserians did not confine themselves to the recovery of the obsolete or half-forgotten word. They made their imitations an excuse for verbal innovations which would not have been permitted in other 'kinds' of poetry. Thus Thomson's streamlets 'bicker' and his rills 'prattle'. We may perhaps attribute the particularity of these 'simple' metaphors, so unusual in the diction of contemporary pastoralism, to the guidance of Spenser.

It is obvious that the imitation of the verse and words of earlier poets will often result in no more than laboured copies of the master's work. But the poems examined in this chapter show that imitation can also be consistent with original composition. Old forms can be used for new effects; forgotten words can enlarge the scope of contemporary diction. The imitation of Milton and Spenser did not hinder poets like Thomson, Collins, and Shenstone. It enabled them to give ready and convincing expression to their poetic purposes.

CHAPTER VIII

IMITATION AND ORIGINAL COMPOSITION
—GRAY

THE last chapter dealt largely with imitation of verse and diction; but as much effort was spent by Augustan poets in imitating the thoughts and expressions of earlier writers. To see in this, as several contemporaries did, evidence of poverty of imagination and to regard it as little better than plagiarism is to take a very limited view. If the power of reasoning leads right-thinking men to the same conclusions in all ages of the world, as was widely assumed—'Whatever is very good sense', said Pope, 'must have been common sense in all times'—then poets must regard themselves as inheritors of a great tradition of thought and feeling which it is their privilege to interpret to their own generation. Their art lies therefore in the expression. Never mind that what they said had oft been said before; there was still a chance that it was ne'er so well expressed as they were expressing it. 'The objects of imitation', wrote Hurd, in his *Discourse on Poetical Imitation* (1757), 'like the materials of human knowledge, are a common stock, which experience furnishes to all men. And it is in the operations of the mind upon them that the glory of poetry, as of science, consists'. 'Glory', suggests the triumphant close of a noble contention; and for regarding imitation in that light there was good classical precedent. When Dryden admitted that the scene between Troilus and Hector in his version of *Troilus and Cressida* was modelled partly on similar scenes in Euripides' *Iphigenia*, Shakespeare's *Julius Cæsar*, and Beaumont and Fletcher's *The Maid's Tragedy*, he concluded his justification with the following passage from Longinus:

We ought not to regard a good imitation as a theft, but as a beautiful idea of him who undertakes to imitate, by forming himself on the invention and the work of another man; for he enters into the lists like a new wrestler, to dispute the prize with the former champion. This sort of emulation, says Hesiod, is honourable, Ἀγαθὴ δ'ἔρις ἐστὶ βρότοισιν—when we combat for victory with a hero, and are not without glory even in our overthrow. Those great men, whom we propose to ourselves as patterns of our imitation, serve us as a torch, which is lifted up before us, to enlighten our passage, and often elevate our thoughts as high as the conception we have of our author's genius.

The best imitative poets often print in footnotes the passages imitated, so as to ensure that the reader will not miss the artistry of the imitation. This was Pope's practice, and his justification may be read in a paper he is believed to have contributed to *The Guardian* (1713; No. 12):

. . . over and above a just Painting of Nature, a learned Reader will find a new Beauty superadded in a happy Imitation of some famous Ancient, as it revives in his Mind the Pleasure he took in his first reading such an Author. Such Copyings as these give that kind of double Delight which we perceive when we look upon the Children of a beautiful Couple; where the Eye is not more charm'd with the Symmetry of the Parts, than the Mind by observing the Resemblance transmitted from Parents to their Offspring, and the mingled Features of the Father and the Mother.

This learned pleasure is to a large degree the delight offered by Gray's poetry, for Gray was an imitator too, not merely of the thoughts and expressions but of the diction and versification of his predecessors. His work is, indeed, a mosaic of 'what oft was thought, but ne'er so well expressed', and much of this mosaic work was consciously designed. Writing of his 'British Ode' ('The Bard') to Bedingfield in 1756, he points out that some words 'are almost stoln from Milton', another passage 'is an imitation of Cowley', a third 'has a near affinity to a line in Shakespeare's King John . . . & there are two lines together in the Epode here pilfer'd from his Julius Cæsar'. 'Do not wonder therefore', he continues, 'if some

Magazine or Review call me Plagiary: I could shew them a hundred more instances, wᶜʰ they never will discover themselves'; and in conclusion he lays stress upon the degree of learning needed for a just appreciation of his work:

. . . one thing I must say, (but this is sacred, & under the seal of confession) there is no Woman, that can take pleasure in this kind of composition. if Parts only & Imagination & Sensibility were required, one might (I doubt not) find them in that Sex full as easily as in our own: but there is a certain measure of learning necessary, & a long acquaintance with the good Writers ancient & modern, wᶜʰ by our injustice is denied to them. and without this they can only catch here & there a florid expression, or a musical rhyme, while the Whole appears to them a wild obscure unedifying jumble.

Gray made some efforts to meet his female readers by quoting a few of his 'originals' in footnotes; but others he must have felt were too familiar, and of some he seems not to have been aware. Popular as *The Rape of the Lock* still is to-day, we must assume that it was even more widely read in the eighteenth century, and that Gray would not need to remind his readers of Belinda's despairing lament over her loss:

> Oh had I rather un-admir'd remain'd
> In some lone Isle, or distant *Northern* Land . . .
> There kept my Charms conceal'd from mortal Eye,
> Like Roses that in Desarts bloom and die,[1]

itself modelled on the second verse of Waller's 'Go lovely rose' —when they read the stanza:

> Full many a gem of purest ray serene,
> The dark unfathom'd caves of ocean bear:
> Full many a flower is born to blush unseen,
> And waste its sweetness on the desert air.

Similarly Gray may have expected his readers to recall one of

[1] iv, 153–6.

the many translations of a famous passage in Lucretius, or Thomson's previous use of it in *Winter*,[1] when they read:

> For them no more the blazing hearth shall burn
> Or busy housewife ply her evening care:
> No children run to lisp their sire's return,
> Or climb his knees the envied kiss to share.

He draws attention to Dante's pilgrim, in the eighth Canto of the *Purgatorio*, listening to the evening bell—'*Che paia il giorno pianger che si muore*',[2] and tells Bedingfield that it is the source of 'the knell of parting day', but he overlooks another source in Dante for the same stanza (*Inferno*, ii. 1–3):

> Lo giorno se n'andava, e l'aer bruno
> toglieva gli animai che sono in terra
> dalle fatiche loro; ed io sol uno . . . ' [3]

and by not quoting his source for 'incense-breathing morn' in Milton ('the humid flowers, that breath'd Their morning incense', *Paradise Lost*, ix. 193) and in Pope ('See Nature hastes her earliest wreaths to bring, With all the incense of the breathing spring', *Messiah*, ll. 23–4), he slightly obscures his meaning for those who do not immediately recall his originals.

Not only does Gray think what had often been thought before, the mood which he expresses in the *Elegy* had often been suggested before, and suggested by the same means. Il Penseroso had long been a favourite figure in eighteenth-century poetry. Readers of Lady Winchilsea's poems knew him well—indeed her famous 'Nocturnal Reverie' might suitably bear the motto 'And leaves the world to darkness and to me' —and in Parnell's 'Night Piece on Death' he is already found

---

[1] In vain for him the officious wife prepares
    The fire fair-blazing and the vestment warm;
    In vain his little children, peeping out
    Into the mingling storm, demand their sire
    With tears of artless innocence.

The same passage from Lucretius (iii. 894–6) was to be imitated again in Collins's most original poem, the 'Popular Superstitions' Ode, ll. 121 ff.

[2] 'that seems to mourn the dying day'.

[3] 'the day was departing, and the dusky air was loosening from their labours the living things that are on earth; and I alone . . .'.

meditating in a graveyard. 'Twilight groves . . . and inter-mingled graves' had formed part of the sympathetic landscape for 'Black Melancholy's' seat in Pope's 'Eloisa to Abelard'; in his *Claremont* (1715) Garth had included an ivy-mantled ruin, a bat, and a 'drowsie Beetle'; and while Gray was at work on his *Elegy*, Thomas Warton had described the pleasures of melancholy in phraseology astonishingly close to Gray's.

Nor was Gray's use of the quatrain for elegiac purposes sufficiently unusual to provoke comment. It is true that for many eighteenth-century readers the quatrain was associated with heroic rather than elegiac poetry through Davenant's epic, *Gondibert*, and Dryden's *Annus Mirabilis;* but by the time the *Elegy* was published in 1751, the practice of Hammond and Shenstone had established the quatrain as the most suitable elegiac measure.

The *Elegy*, then, was in no respects an unusual poem, but Gray there preserved what is of lasting value in the graveyard sentiment of the time. Part of his success lies in his reconcilia-tion of the general and the particular. The images had almost all been used before in this context, but the poet had seen them anew. Indeed so 'particular' is the beech 'that wreathes its old fantastic roots so high', so peculiar is it to the woods at Burnham, that Gray was censured by a contemporary for not recording those features only which characterize the species. The critic might have taken as much exception to the 'straw-built shed', an equally unusual feature of the landscape. It is in part this freshness of vision and in part the rhetorical skill shown in varying caesura and accent that gives life to these divine truisms to which every bosom returns an echo.

Gray's Pindaric odes have never received such widespread approval as the *Elegy*. 'We are not at all popular', Gray told Wharton, soon after their publication in 1757, 'the great objection is obscurity, no body knows what we would be at'. This accounts for the peevish 'Advertisement' prefixed to the edition of 1768:

When the Author first published this and the following Ode, he was advised, even by his Friends, to subjoin some few explanatory

Notes; but had too much respect for the understanding of his Readers to take that liberty.

But obscurity, as Burke pointed out, was not incompatible with the Sublime, and 'The Progress of Poesy' and 'The Bard' are the most 'sublime' pieces Gray wrote. The effect of the Welsh bards, Gray was told[1] is to 'transport, enrapture, alarm, astonish, and confound us'. It was so; and it is fortunate that Mason, Gray's biographer, preserved the comments on these two odes of 'an ingenious person, who sent Mr. Gray his remarks anonymously', for this critic exhibits a model response to the Sublime.

This abrupt execration [he writes of the first strophe of 'The Bard'] plunges the reader into that sudden fearful perplexity which is designed to predominate through the whole. The irresistible violence of the prophet's passions bears him away, who, as he is unprepared by a formal ushering in of the speaker, is unfortified against the impressions of his poetical phrenzy, and overpowered by them, as sudden thunders strike the deepest;

and again:

It is . . . a beauty that runs throughout the whole composition, that the historical events are briefly sketched out by a few striking circumstances, in which the poet's office of rather exciting and directing, than satisfying the reader's imagination, is perfectly observed. Such abrupt hints, resembling the several fragments of a vast ruin, suffer not the mind to be raised to the utmost pitch, by one image of horror, but that instantaneously a second and a third are presented to it, and the affection is still uniformly supported.

We might have expected the anonymous critic to admire the contrast of the beautiful and the sublime at the close of the second antistrophe of 'The Bard',[2] and the sublimity of blinding light, infinite space, and uncontrollable power which Gray uses

[1]By Beattie in a letter dated 16th February, 1768.

[2]Fair laughs the Morn, and soft the Zephyr blows,
    While proudly riding o'er the azure realm
    In gallant trim the gilded Vessel goes;
    Youth on the prow, and Pleasure at the helm;
    Regardless of the sweeping Whirlwind's sway,
    That, hush'd in grim repose, expects his evening-prey.

to describe the spirit of Milton's and of Dryden's work in 'The Progress of Poesy':

> Nor second He, that rode sublime
> Upon the seraph-wings of Extasy,
> The secrets of th' Abyss to spy.
> He pass'd the flaming bounds of Place and Time:
> The living Throne, the saphire-blaze,
> Where Angels tremble, while they gaze,
> He saw; but blasted with excess of light,
> Closed his eyes in endless night.
> Behold where Dryden's less presumptuous car
> Wide o'er the fields of Glory bear
> Two Coursers of etherial race,
> With necks in thunder cloath'd, and long-resounding pace.

'The flaming bounds of Place and Time' is a bold expression, and so is 'with necks in thunder cloath'd'. As though to justify them, Gray reminds us that the first is adapted from Lucretius and the second from the Book of Job. Whether it was his purpose to justify them, or whether (in Lord David Cecil's words) 'he wishes to enhance the effect of his own lines by setting astir in the mind memories of those great poets of whom he feels himself the heir', this passage provides one more example to show both how learned and how 'imitative' Gray's poetry is.

When studying his diction we find still further evidence of this and of the essentially traditional character of Gray's poetry. As a young man of twenty-five just starting to write verse, he was incited to express his views on poetic diction by his friend West, to whom he had sent a fragment of a tragedy he had been writing. West's comment was that the style was too antiquated. 'I will not decide', he says, 'what style is fit for our English stage; but I should rather choose one that bordered upon [Addison's] Cato, than upon Shakespeare'. By all means try to imitate Shakespeare's strokes of nature and his force in painting characters, is West's advice, but preserve at the same time our own language. Gray disagreed. 'The language of the age', he told West[1], 'is never the language of poetry'. Poetry, he says, has a language of its own to which almost every poet has added something; and he proceeds to illustrate his remark by citing some of Dryden's Elizabethan borrowings ('a *roundelay* of love' —'in proud *array*'—'his *boon* was granted'—*'wayward* but wise'—*'smouldring* flames'). Gray's point, presumably, was that the language had been enriched by borrowings of what to him seemed half-forgotten words. He himself has taken Shakespeare as authority, he tells West; 'Every word in him is a picture': and in imitation of Shakespeare's metaphoric style he has ventured upon *'silken* son of *dalliance—drowsier* pretensions— wrinkled *beldams—arched* the hearer's brow and *riveted* his eyes in *fearful extasie'*, expressions which he fears may be too faulty. It is some measure of the distance we have travelled since 1740 that to-day we should find nothing startling in any of Dryden's or of Gray's borrowings. We have grown tired of 'boons' and 'beldams', and the 'arched' brow and 'riveted' eye have become the clichés of the careless novelist; perhaps only the 'roundelay of Love' and the 'silken sons of dalliance' still retain any of their Elizabethan flavour. How difficult is it then to appreciate the colour of these recovered words in their eighteenth-century contexts, to recognize the antique gesture of Pope's 'The Pomp, the Pageantry, the proud *Array*'[2] or the choiceness of the unusual in Gray's 'Mutt'ring his *wayward* fancies he would rove'.[3]

Gray enjoyed recovering words as much as the Spenserians. 'Dreary' and 'aghast', which they had recorded in their glossaries, he finds a place for in the Pindaric odes ('the dreary sky', *P. of P.*, l. 51; 'stood aghast in speechless trance', *Bard*, l. 13); 'havoc' and 'hurtles' he found in Shakespeare and retrieved ('long years of havoc', *Bard*, l. 85; 'Iron-sleet of arrowy shower Hurtles in the darken'd air', *The Fatal Sisters*, ll. 3, 4); and he seems to have been responsible for at least one

---

[1] 8th April, 1742; *Letters*, ed. Toynbee-Whibley (Oxford, 1935), p. 192. He was to express a somewhat different view at the end of his life (see his letter to Beattie, 8th March, 1771; ed.cit., p. 1168), but that was some little time after he had ceased to write poetry.

[2] *January and May*, l. 308.

[3] *Elegy*, l. 106.

invention much vulgarized since his day, the adjective 'thriliing' ('thrilling Fears', *P. of P.*, l. 93; 'the thrilling verse that wakes the Dead', *The Descent of Odin*, l. 24).

The majority of these recovered words are to be found in Gray's Celtic odes; and that is what we should expect. The strangeness of subject demanded strangeness of diction. 'You have made every thing magical and dreadful', wrote Beattie to Gray of *The Fatal Sisters;* and as if recognizing that Gray's diction helped to achieve this effect, he immediately added: 'Your choice of words on this, as on every other occasion, is the happiest that can be'. But Gray bestowed equal care upon the diction of his other pieces. We have already had occasion to notice his admiration for Shakespeare's metaphorical style, and it was that model which Gray always kept before him. In the *Ode on the Spring* the beech 'o'er-canopies the glade', and the busy murmur of insects 'glows' through the 'peopled air'; the gales in the 'Ode on a Distant Prospect of Eton College' are 'redolent of joy', and Envy 'inly gnaws the secret heart'. Johnson found this language 'too luxuriant' and censured Gray for thinking 'his language more poetical as it was more remote from common use'. It is not surprising that Wordsworth should have shared this opinion, since his view was that 'the language of a large portion of every good poem . . . must necessarily, except with reference to the metre, in no respect differ from that of good prose'. To illustrate this view Wordsworth used, in the preface to *Lyrical Ballads* (1800), 'a short composition of Gray, who was at the head of those who, by their reasonings, have attempted to widen the space of separation betwixt Prose and Metrical composition, and was more than any other man curiously elaborate in the structure of his own poetic diction'. The piece he chose was Gray's sonnet on the death of his friend West (1742):

> In vain to me the smileing Mornings shine,
>   And redning Phoebus lifts his golden Fire:
> The Birds in vain their amorous Descant joyn;
>   Or chearful Fields resume their green Attire:
> These Ears, alas! for other Notes repine,
>   *A different Object do these Eyes require.*

> *My lonely Anguish melts no Heart, but mine;*
>   *And in my Breast the imperfect Joys expire.*
> Yet Morning smiles the busy Race to chear.
>   And new-born Pleasure brings to happier Men:
> The Fields to all their wonted Tribute bear:
>   To warm their little Loves the Birds complain:
> *I fruitless mourn to him, that cannot hear,*
>   *And weep the more because I weep in vain.*

Wordsworth pronounced that 'the only part of this Sonnet
which is of any value is the lines printed in Italics', the language
of which 'does in no respect differ from that of prose'. But is the
issue as simple as that? The lines printed in italics are certainly
most moving, but they are the more effective because their
prosaic language contrasts with the elaborate diction of the
remaining lines. And the contrast in diction was surely designed
to set off the contrast in theme. General Nature, Gray seems
to say, looks the same to every man: it is no respecter of an
individual's grief. The conventional descriptions are therefore
used to represent what all see and hear alike, and the simple
language of the heart to express what the individual feels.

Poetry like this is neither spontaneous nor tries to look
spontaneous. All its effects are calculated, even its frenzies. It
is highly sophisticated; but practitioners like Gray never forgot
that however much the intellect, the memory, and the ear are
delighted the supreme appeal is to the heart.

CHAPTER IX

JOHNSON

'THE Age of Johnson' is a phrase which has gained almost as wide a currency as 'The Augustan Age'. It may therefore be thought incongruous to include Johnson himself among the Augustans. But if Thomson was an Augustan both in spirit and in time, and if Gray has Augustan affinities, then Johnson too, who was a mere nine years younger than Thomson and seven years older than Gray, may be claimed for the earlier age. In the next chapter we shall see that there were signs in the seventeen-sixties of a change in taste, of a new age beginning. By that time Johnson's reputation was made, and had been sealed in 1762 by the grant of a pension 'not . . . for any thing you are to do', as the Prime Minister explained, 'but for what you have done'. In fact he was then already beyond middle age, and could at last afford to take life a little more easily. In 1763 he and Boswell had met for the first time, and it is largely to Boswell's records of their subsequent meetings that we owe our conception of Johnson as the predominating figure in the literary society of his day; but we must remember that he owed his position in 'the Age of Johnson' to what he had done in a former age,[1] and that such an irrepressible lion-hunter as Boswell would not have troubled to seek Johnson out unless he had already been famous. These, then, are some of the grounds for including Johnson among the Augustans.

His reputation had been made by slow degrees. Just when it was that he first decided to fight his way in London by his

---

[1] Smollett was already referring to Johnson as 'that great CHAM of literature' in 1759 (Boswell, *Life*, ed. Hill-Powell, 1934, i. 348).

literature and his wit[1] we do not know—several passages of his
life before he met Boswell are still obscure to us—but it was
in 1734 that he wrote to Edward Cave, who had founded *The
Gentleman's Magazine* in 1731, offering 'on reasonable terms,
sometimes to fill a column'. He suggested 'poems, inscriptions,
&c. never printed before . . . likewise short literary dissertations
in Latin or English, critical remarks on authors ancient or
modern, forgotten poems that deserve revival, or loose pieces'.
At that time Johnson was twenty-five years old. Much of the
five years passed since leaving Oxford he had spent in trying
to place himself as a schoolmaster in his native Midlands; but
he had been writing too. While lodging with a school friend in
Birmingham (1732–3) he had contributed a series of essays
(which no longer survive) to *The Birmingham Journal* and had
started his translation from the French of Father Lobo's
Voyage to Abyssinia (published 1734), whose preface shows that
his capacity for moral generalization was already formed and
that his prose style had already acquired some of its
characteristic rhythms.

Nothing came immediately of his application to Cave, and
for the next few years Johnson still tried to gain by school-
teaching a livelihood for himself and the middle-aged widow
he had married, while at the same time he continued to write.
In the intervals of teaching he had composed most of his blank
verse tragedy, *Irene*, and it was in an attempt to secure its
stage-performance that he paid his first visit to London in
1737. He secured nothing better than promises, but a second
approach to Cave met with more success. Cave accepted for
publication in *The Gentleman's Magazine* a Latin ode addressed
to him by Johnson, approved Johnson's scheme for translating
from the Italian Father Paul Sarpi's *History of the Council of
Trent*, and undertook to print Johnson's first important poem,
London,[2] if Dodsley would publish it. Several commissions
from Cave followed, the most important being the writing of

[1] *Life*, i. 74.
[2] An imitation of Juvenal's third satire. This form, in which the words
of a classical poem were closely applied to modern conditions, had become
popular in the late seventeenth century. The best examples are Pope's
Imitations of Horace (1733–8) and Johnson's *Vanity of Human Wishes*.

Parliamentary Debates[1] for *The Gentleman's Magazine* from
1741 to 1744 and, if one report be true, the editing of that journal
on Cave's behalf. By the early seventeen-forties he had become
established as a bookseller's hack, but it was quite clear that he
was well above the average in ability. He could be relied upon
for biography and for translation as well as for work, such as the
essay on the origin and importance of small tracts and fugitive
pieces prefixed to the *Harleian Miscellany* (1743), involving a
good grasp of the general principles of scholarship. In fact he
was already beginning to demonstrate the truth of his friend
Sir Joshua Reynolds's judgment[2] that he had a mind always
ready for use. Reynolds was thinking of Johnson's power as a
conversationalist, but the remark has a wider relevance. When
he was a lad of sixteen Johnson had been advised by his cousin
Cornelius Ford, to 'obtain some general principles of every
science; he [Ford continued] who can talk only on one subject,
or act only in one department, is seldom wanted, and perhaps
never wished for; while the man of general knowledge can
often benefit, and always please'.[3] As Mrs. Piozzi reflected, who
recorded these remarks,[4] 'No man surely ever followed [this
advice] more exactly'. His reading in his early years had been

[1]Johnson was never inside either House. At a time when the reporting of
Parliamentary Debates was illegal, he relied at best on an account of who
had spoken and the line of argument the speaker adopted. But frequently
he was compelled to have recourse to his imagination. The speeches rarely
give the impression of the cut and thrust of debate, though the retort upon
the elder Horace Walpole, which Johnson credited to Pitt, is lively enough:
> 'Sir, the atrocious crime of being a young man, which the honourable
> gentleman has with such spirit and decency charged upon me, I shall
> neither attempt to palliate nor to deny, but content myself with wishing
> that I may be one of those whose follies may cease with their youth,
> & not of that number who are ignorant in spite of experience'.

[2]*Johnsonian Miscellanies*, ed. Hill (Oxford, 1897), ii. 220.

[3]ibid., i. 155.

[4]Mrs. Piozzi recorded another and possibly more authentic version in her
note-book:
> Nealy Ford . . . advised him to study the Principles of every thing, that
> a general Acquaintance with Life might be the Consequence of his
> Enquiries—Learn said he the leading Precognita of all things—no need
> per[haps] to turn over leaf by leaf; but grasp the Trunk hard only, and
> you will shake all the Branches. *Thraliana*, ed. K. C. Balderstone
> (Oxford, 1942), p. 171.

voracious and wide without any set plan of study such as Milton followed. He told Boswell that he had never persisted in any such plan for two days together, but he had looked into a great many books, and had acquired a large stock of knowledge. He was exceptionally well and widely informed, and this information stood him in excellent stead in the many journalistic commissions on which he relied for his living. In 1756 he wrote a preface to a *Dictionary of Trade and Commerce* by Richard Rolt. When asked by Boswell whether he knew much of Rolt and his work, Johnson exclaimed: 'Sir, I never saw the man, and never read the book. The booksellers wanted a Preface to a Dictionary of Trade and Commerce. I knew very well what such a Dictionary should be, and I wrote a Preface accordingly'. In much the same spirit he contributed prefaces or composed dedications for such books as Payne's *New Tables of Interest* (1758) and his *Introduction to Geometry* (1767), Kennedy's *Complete System of Astronomical Chronology* (1763), for which he also seems to have written the noble concluding paragraph, and *The World displayed; or, a Curious Collection of Voyages and Travels* (1759–61).[1]

Such fugitive pieces admirably exhibit the power of Johnson's well-informed and ready mind, and his ability to shake all the branches by a firm grasp on the trunk. But if Johnson had spent all his time upon them, we should have sympathized with the implied reproach in a letter from his old Lichfield friend, Gilbert Walmesley to David Garrick (3rd November, 1746):

When you see Mr. Johnson pray [give] him my compliments, and tell him I esteem him as a great genius—quite lost both to himself and the world.

By 1746 he had already published at least two works of the first importance, his poem *London* (1738) and the *Life of Savage* (1744), and he was meditating greater things, an edition of Shakespeare and an English Dictionary. The edition of

[1] Our knowledge of this aspect of Johnson's work was much increased by Mr. A. T. Hazen, who in *Samuel Johnson's Prefaces & Dedications* (New Haven, 1937) reprinted most of these fugitive publications with ample bibliographical description.

Shakespeare was not to appear for another twenty years (1765), though the first proposals for it accompanied his *Miscellaneous Observations on the Tragedy of Macbeth* (1745), and the *Dictionary* he had long had in mind before Dodsley, the bookseller, first mentioned the scheme to him. Even if we did not know this from Johnson's own words, we should be justified in assuming from the opening sentences of his *Plan of a Dictionary of the English Language* (1747) that he had given the scheme long and weighty consideration. Those shrewd men the booksellers knew that Johnson could do greater things than the hack work they had given him in the late thirties; they were making sure for their part that a great genius was not lost to the world. Nor need we doubt that the genius himself was ready to co-operate with them for that purpose.

The *Dictionary* and the edition of Shakespeare are Johnson's two greatest contributions to scholarship. He was not a scholar in the sense that Bentley or that Thomas Warton were scholars, for his irregular habits as a reader prevented him from making a prolonged study of a special field of knowledge. But few men have had a better understanding of the methods and purposes of scholarship. Taking the *Oxford Dictionary* as our standard of what a dictionary should be, we may look back at Johnson's work and find that he has anticipated the Oxford lexicographers at almost every point. To some matters he attaches more importance than we do now: to others which we consider important he pays little attention. For lack of a phonetic alphabet he can offer small help on pronunciation; and though well equipped to deal with words of Romance derivation, he could do no more than trust to Junius and Skinner for Germanic words. But what he has thought about is remarkable nevertheless. He proposes to deal not merely with orthography but also 'to trace back the orthography of different ages, and show by what gradations the word departed from its original'; to cite authorities for the use of words; to name, where possible, the first users of new words and the last to admit those that are obsolete; to provide not merely the present meanings of words but to show how the present meaning has been reached. And in one sentence he has written what might have been taken for the motto of the *Oxford Dictionary:*

By this method every word will have its history, and the reader will be informed of the gradual changes of the language, and have before his eyes the rise of some words and the fall of others.

But though he had a conception of 'a new English dictionary on historical principles', as the *Oxford Dictionary* was originally called, that was not Johnson's primary intention. His proposal was 'to preserve the purity, and ascertain the meaning of our English idiom'; and the historical instrument was to serve this standardizing purpose, for 'by tracing . . . every word to its original, and not admitting, but with great caution any of which no original can be found, we shall secure our language from being overrun with cant, from being crowded with low terms, the spawn of folly or affectation, which arise from no just principles of speech, and of which therefore no legitimate derivation can be shown'. This, as he later admitted, was the dream of a poet 'doomed at last to wake a lexicographer'. Experience was to teach him, and in the Preface to the *Dictionary* (1755) he was to admit, that the lexicographer deserved to be derided who could 'imagine that his dictionary can embalm his language, and secure it from corruption and decay', and he adds, dwelling characteristically on the moral aspect of his work, '[or] that it is in his power to change sublunary nature, and clear the world at once from folly, vanity, and affectation'. His interest in the historical aspect of his work seems to have quickened during its progress. Though in his preface he notices some 'spots of barbarity impressed so deep in the English language, that criticism can never wash them away', the attitude which experience taught him to adopt was 'to proceed with a scholar's reverence for antiquity' and 'to collect examples and authorities from the writers before the restoration, whose works I regard as *the wells of English undefiled*'.[1]

---

[1]But he did not eschew quotations from contemporaries; see A. W. Read, 'The Contemporary Quotations in Johnson's Dictionary', *ELH*, ii (1935), 246–51.

Johnson found himself unable to accomplish in his *Dictionary* all he set out to perform, and the weaknesses evident in the *Plan* were not removed in the work itself. By modern standards the guidance on pronunciation is poor—though improvements were made in a later edition (1773) and a distinction was attempted between 'solemn' and colloquial pronunciations—the etymology is inaccurate, and the quotations lack dates and references. Some of the definitions have been found incorrect, prejudiced, or verbose, but only the most assiduous reader of the *Dictionary* would discover more examples to amuse him than the handful which entertained Johnson's contemporaries. Johnson intended the wryness of his definition of 'lexicographer'[1] and the sarcasm of his definition of 'favourite'[2] to please those who found them. But for those who laughed at his definitions of 'cough'[3] and 'network'[4], he had his answers. 'To explain', he writes,

requires the use of terms less abstruse than that which is to be explained, and such terms cannot always be found. . . . Sometimes easier words are changed into harder . . . for, the easiest word, whatever it be, can never be translated into one more easy. But easiness and difficulty are merely relative; and if the present prevalence of our language should invite foreigners to this dictionary, many will be assisted by those words which now seem only to increase or produce obscurity. For this reason I have endeavoured frequently to join a Teutonick and Roman interpretation . . . that every learner of English may be assisted by his own tongue;

or if that pistol misses fire, the reader is knocked down with the butt end of it:

a few wild blunders, and risible absurdities, from which no work of such multiplicity was ever free, may for a time furnish folly with laughter, and harden ignorance into contempt; but useful diligence will at last prevail. . . .

[1]'A writer of dictionaries; a harmless drudge'.

[2]'One chosen as a companion by a superiour; a mean wretch whose whole business is by any means to please'.

[3]'A convulsion of the lungs vellicated by some sharp serosity'.

[4]'Any thing reticulated or decussated, at equal distances, with interstices between the intersections'.

In spite of blemishes, the *Dictionary* was greatly superior to any previous English dictionary, and served as a basis for other men's revisions until as late as 1883. Nor is it merely a curiosity to-day; for, as any editor of an eighteenth-century text knows, it will sometimes serve better than the *Oxford Dictionary* to fix the precise meaning a word held two hundred years ago.

Work upon the *Dictionary* had led Johnson to wider reading in Elizabethan literature than was common in his day. He had long been convinced that 'to make a true estimate of the abilities and merit of a writer, it is always necessary to examine the genius of his age, and the opinions of his contemporaries',[1] in which he was at one with the best scholarship of the day; and in a letter to Thomas Warton on the publication of his *Observations on Spenser's Fairy Queen* (1754) he shows his recognition of one purpose which his *Dictionary* might serve:

You have shewn [he writes] to all, who shall hereafter attempt the study of our ancient authours, the way to success; by directing them to the perusal of the books which those authours had read. . . . The reason why the authours, which are yet read, of the sixteenth century, are so little understood, is, that they are read alone; and no help is borrowed from those who lived with them, or before them. Some part of this ignorance I hope to remove by my book, which now draws towards its end. . . .

In one particular, then, he was well qualified to turn from English lexicography to the editing of Shakespeare's plays: his work on the *Dictionary* had given him this great advantage over previous editors that, having a better understanding of the changes in meaning and in grammar since the sixteenth century and having a wider knowledge of Elizabethan literature, he could explain to eighteenth-century readers more of the difficulties in Shakespeare's plays which were in no way strange to Shakespeare's audience. This advantage he pressed in his *Proposals for Printing the Dramatick Works of William Shakespeare* (1756), a pamphlet which shows how fully he understood the principles upon which an edition should be undertaken. His account of the sources of the corruption of

[1] *Miscellaneous Observations on the Tragedy of Macbeth* (1745).

Shakespeare's text needs some modification, but his remarks on the method to be employed in restoring the text and on the dangers of conjecture are essentially sound. Here, said a recent editor of Shakespeare,[1] is 'the first hint of a rational study of Shakespeare's text. . . . If only some editors who followed him had pondered over the significance of his words, how much trouble they might have saved themselves and of how many superfluous footnotes would editions of Shakespeare have been relieved'.

If the text and the annotation (in spite of the strong common sense shown in clearing syntactical obscurities) are disappointing after the promise of the Proposals, the Preface to the edition (1765) gave Johnson the opportunity of exercising a talent he had already exercised in the Preface to the *Dictionary* and of which he was fully conscious: 'There are two things', he once remarked, 'which I am confident I can do very well: one is an introduction to any literary work, stating what it is to contain, and how it should be executed in the most perfect manner; the other is a conclusion, shewing from various causes why the execution has not been equal to what the authour promised to himself and to the publick'. But there are other things in the Preface besides. The luminousness of the aphorisms has scarcely been surpassed, and the vigour of the defence of Shakespeare for not observing the unities shows the liberal tradition of English classical criticism at its best; yet some readers will prefer to turn to the last few pages where Johnson examines the performance of his predecessors and presents his own experience as an editor. What could be better than:

I have always suspected that the reading is right, which requires many words to prove it wrong; and the emendation wrong, that cannot without so much labour appear to be right,

or:

Particular passages are cleared by notes, but the general effect of the work is weakened. The mind is refrigerated by interruption; the thoughts are diverted from the principal subject; the reader is

[1] Ronald B. McKerrow, *The Treatment of Shakespeare's Text by his earlier Editors* (London, 1933), pp. 27-8.

weary, he suspects not why; and at last throws away the book, which
he has too diligently studied,

or:

I could have written longer notes, for the art of writing notes is not
of difficult attainment. The work is performed, first by railing at
the stupidity, negligence, ignorance, and asinine tastelessness of
former editors, and shewing, from all that goes before and all that
follows, the inelegance and absurdity of the old reading; then by
proposing something, which to superficial readers would seem
specious, but which the editor rejects with indignation; then by
producing the true reading, with a long paraphrase, and concluding
with loud acclamations on the discovery, and a sober wish for the
advancement and prosperity of genuine criticism.

No one should start to edit a text without first reading the
concluding pages of Johnson's preface.

Johnson could not have supported himself from 1747 to
1765 on the proceeds of the *Dictionary* and *Shakespeare* alone.
It was in 1750 that he started to revive the periodical essay by
publishing *The Rambler* twice a week for the space of two
years;[1] he superintended and contributed to fifteen numbers of
The Literary Magazine in 1756; and from 1758 to 1760 he
wrote a weekly essay called 'The Idler' for *The Universal
Chronicle*, a more lively work than *The Rambler* and one which
Jane Austen was to choose sixty years later for the light reading
of her favourite heroine in *Mansfield Park*. These are a few of his
activities during the years when he was working at the
Dictionary and the *Shakespeare:* he also wrote numerous
reviews as well as two other major works, his second verse
imitation of Juvenal, *The Vanity of Human Wishes* (1747), and
Rasselas (1759), a tale composed in the evenings of one week
to pay for the cost of his mother's funeral. To have written
The Rambler alone was a remarkable feat for a man who had
always to fight against indolence, but the feat was responsible
for a lack of variety in his periodical essays which most readers
acknowledge. Already in *Rambler*, 23, he mentions that
he had received several remonstrances. He was too solemn,
too serious, too dictatorial, he was not sprightly, he did not take

[1]He wrote all but 7 of the 208 numbers.

sufficient notice of the clubs of the town, and his naked moral precepts needed setting off with characters and examples. Such were the complaints; and Johnson ignored them. But he paid the penalty with a sale which never exceeded 500 copies.[1] He admitted in the final number that he had 'never been much a favourite of the publick'; yet it was in a mood of tempered satisfaction that he looked back on his labours and, in doing so, summarized his policy. He had 'laboured to refine our language to grammatical purity' and had, he thought, 'added to the elegance of its construction, and something to the harmony of its cadence'. He had written a few papers 'of which the highest excellence is harmless merriment', and some had been devoted to criticism. But his principal design had been 'to inculcate wisdom or piety', and he therefore hoped to be numbered 'among the writers who have given ardour to virtue, and confidence to truth'. Addison's intention in *The Spectator* had been no less moral, but he had been prepared to insinuate his advice. Yet though Johnson had little use for the arts which Addison employed to sweeten his teaching, there will always be some readers who prefer Johnson's vigour and the impression he conveys of speaking from hard-won experience. Johnson's morality is never bookish; it is confirmed by books, but it is not drawn from them. Indeed he frequently recurs to the diseases of personality incident to those who live too much with books, and the dangers and disappointments which follow those who judge the world by what they read. The advice Johnson gives to the young scholar in *The Vanity of Human Wishes* is:

> Deign on the passing world to turn thine eyes,
> And pause awhile from letters to be wise.

The young heir in *Rambler*, 177, who decided to retire from the world to his library, found after some years that his mind was contracted and stiffened by solitude:

My ease and elegance were sensibly impaired; I was no longer able to accommodate myself with readiness to the accidental current of

[1] He attracted more readers when *The Rambler* was reissued in volume form: a fourth edition was published in 1756, and six more appeared before Johnson's death.

conversation; my notions grew particular and paradoxical, and my phraseology formal and unfashionable; I spoke on common occasions the language of books. My quickness of apprehension, and celerity of reply, had entirely deserted me: when I delivered my opinion, or detailed my knowledge, I was bewildered by an unseasonable interrogatory, disconcerted by any slight opposition, and overwhelmed and lost in dejection when the smallest advantage was gained against me in dispute;

and the young man fresh from college is given some excellent counsel in *Rambler*, 173, when he is dismayed to find that the world at large considers him (to use our modern slang) a 'highbrow'.

The distinction between life as we find it and those illusions which books and theory foster is further developed in *Rasselas*.[1] The prince finds that happiness cannot be obtained in a region where every desire is immediately granted; that philosophers may discourse like angels, but they live like men; that contrary to the view that happiness is to be found in solitude rather than in public life, the hermit himself discovers by experience that his mind is distracted by doubts and his fancy riots in scenes of folly. But most striking of all is the experience of the learned astronomer, who had spent forty years 'in unwearied attention to the motions and appearances of the celestial bodies', a man of vast comprehension, capacious and retentive memory, methodical discourse, and clear expression, and of integrity and benevolence equal to his learning. Here surely was a happy man; but when Imlac, the companion of Rasselas, had gained his confidence he found the astronomer grieving under the weight of his responsibility for regulating the weather, as he supposed he could, for the benefit of mankind. 'Few can attain this man's knowledge', is Imlac's comment, 'and few practise his virtues; but all may suffer his calamity. Of the uncertainties of our present state, the most dreadful and alarming is the uncertain continuance of human reason'. It was a dread which Imlac shared with his creator, for Johnson, like the mad astronomer, was also afflicted with what he calls

[1] The same distinction was to become the favourite theme of one of Dr. Johnson's later admirers, Jane Austen.

'the dangerous prevalence of imagination'. His tragedy was that he could not always take the advice he placed in Imlac's mouth:

> Open your heart to the influence of the light, which from time to time breaks in on you: when scruples importune you, which you in your lucid moments know to be vain, do not stand to parley, but fly to business . . . and keep this thought always prevalent, that you are only one atom of the mass of humanity, and have neither such virtue nor vice, as that you should be singled out for supernatural favours or afflictions.

The reason why the morality of *Rasselas* and *The Rambler* continues to move us, commonplace as it so often appears to be, is because it is rooted deep in Johnson's own experience. He himself had tested the efficacy of what he taught.

We have seen that with the grant of his pension in 1762 Johnson could afford to relax his efforts. There was still the *Shakespeare* to finish; he was still prepared to write a preface, a dedication, or a review, correct a copy of verses—the noble conclusion (ll. 429–38) he supplied to Goldsmith's *Traveller* (1764) was written at this time—and he could still be persuaded by the booksellers to undertake a larger work such as the *Lives of the Poets;* but he was no longer prepared to admit that the public had a claim upon him. When George III asked him in 1767 if he was then writing anything, he replied that he had pretty well told the world what he knew and that he had done his part as a writer. He had previously expressed the same opinion in more forcible terms to Goldsmith and Boswell:

> No, Sir, I am not obliged to do any more. No man is obliged to do as much as he can do. A man is to have part of his life to himself. . . . A physician, who has practised long in a great city, may be excused if he retires to a small town, and takes less practice. Now, Sir, the good I can do by my conversation bears the same proportion to the good I can do by my writings, that the practice of a physician, retired to a small town, does to his practice in a great city.[1]

This shows, as his most recent biographer, Mr. Krutch, remarks,[2] that 'he had by now adopted talk as a vocation as

[1] *Life*, ii. 15.
[2] J. W. Krutch, *Samuel Johnson* (New York, 1944), p. 338.

well as an amusement'. There were limitations in doing good
by talk other than the physical limitation of influence. There
were the scarcely resistible charms of 'talking for victory' when,
as Boswell remarked, 'exulting in his intellectual strength and
dexterity, he could . . . be the greatest sophist that ever
contended in the lists of declamation'. And there were the
limitations of his audience. Johnson needed a man like Burke
to call forth all his powers, or a man like Boswell to 'feed' him
with topics, for as Sir William Forbes told Boswell, 'I derive
more from Dr. Johnson's admirable discussions [recorded in
Boswell's journals] than I should be able to draw from his
personal conversation; for, I suppose there is not a man in the
world to whom he discloses his sentiments so freely as to
yourself'.[1] Yet allowing for these limitations, Johnson was
justified in the estimate of what his conversation could do. It
was not merely that in conversation he could offer advice, as
when, after pulverizing young Sir John Lade for asking
whether he would advise him to marry—'I would advise no
man to marry, Sir, who is not likely to propagate understanding'
—Johnson relented and 'laid himself out in a dissertation [on
marriage] so useful, so elegant, so founded on the true knowledge of human life, and so adorned with beauty of sentiment,
that no one ever recollected the offence, except to rejoice in its
consequences';[2] it was not merely that he could offer advice,
he had also (in Sir Joshua Reynolds's phrase) 'the faculty of
teaching inferior minds the art of thinking'. He was prepared
to exercise this faculty only if his audience was deferential; but
given that deference, he could brush from the minds of his
companions a great deal of rubbish and show them how to
apply generalizations to their own purposes. When every
allowance has been made for the forcibleness of his expression,
and the tone of authority he gave to his dicta, it was surely the
play of his imagination on a vast variety of topics which
impressed his teaching upon the mind, and which still impresses
us to-day. Sometimes the readiness of his imagery would show
itself in a flash of wit as when he told Boswell that 'a woman's

[1] *Life*, iii. 208.
[2] Piozzi, *Anecdotes* (*Johnsonian Miscellanies*, ed. G. B. Hill, 1897, i. 213 f.).

preaching is like a dog walking on his hinder legs. It is not done well; but you are surprized to find it done at all'; but it was also employed for more extensive analogy as when he used the evidence of the recent conquest of Canada to support the evidences of Christianity:

It is always easy to be on the negative side. If a man were now to deny that there is salt upon the table, you could not reduce him to an absurdity. Come, let us try this a little further. I deny that Canada is taken, and I can support my denial by pretty good arguments. The French are a much more numerous people than we; and it is not likely that they would allow us to take it. "But the ministry have assured us, in all the formality of the Gazette, that it is taken."—Very true. But the ministry have put us to an enormous expence by the war in America, and it is their interest to persuade us that we have got something for our money.—"But the fact is confirmed by thousands of men who were at the taking of it."—Ay, but these men have still more interest in deceiving us. They don't want that you should think the French have beat them, but that they have beat the French. Now suppose you should go over and find that it is really taken, that would only satisfy yourself; for when you come home we will not believe you. We will say, you have been bribed.—Yet, Sir, notwithstanding all these plausible objections, we have no doubt that Canada is really ours. Such is the weight of common testimony. How much stronger are the evidences of the Christian religion?[1]

The delight Johnson here takes in playing with his original conception and supporting the weaker side of the argument is clear and is characteristic of the man, but while he frolics he never forgets his main purpose of arguing for the strength of Christian evidences.

The same note of authority that we hear in Johnson's conversations we hear also in *The Lives of the Poets*. Mr. Eliot remarks[2] that Johnson's style in that book 'reads often like the writing of a man who is more habituated to talking than to writing', and, indeed, many of his dicta can be quite accurately matched with remarks which Boswell had recorded several years earlier. Some of the pleasure in *The Lives of the Poets* is

[1] *Life*, i. 428.
[2] *The Use of Poetry and the Use of Criticism* (London, 1933), p. 64.

derived from the robust expression of prejudices which delights us in Johnson's conversation. It is the physician retired to a small town who remarks of Congreve's *Incognita*, 'I would rather praise it than read it', and of Shenstone's *Pastoral Ballad*, 'an intelligent reader acquainted with the scenes of real life sickens at the mention of the *crook*, the *pipe*, the *sheep*, and the *kids*'. But though these and other dicta like them might be dubbed as provincialisms, the physician had not forgotten that he had practised long in a great city; he never fails to accept the responsibility which criticism of the greatest poems thrusts upon him.

It should not be forgotten that Johnson was originally engaged to write 'little Lives, and little Prefaces, to a little edition of *The English Poets*'. The work was conceived on a quite small scale; and, though it grew upon his hands, in the critical sections he rarely attempted formal treatises. A poem of the outstanding importance of *Paradise Lost* demanded methodical treatment, and Johnson accordingly discussed it under the traditional headings of scheme, fabric, and senti- ments; but such treatment of a poem is exceptional and serves to emphasize, by contrast, the almost casual nature of the work. He throws off hints and observations, but rarely stops to elaborate them. Just as his treatment of *Paradise Lost* shows that he understood 'regular' criticism, criticism conducted in accordance with the 'rules' of poetry, so his remarks on Denham's *Cooper's Hill* and on Pope's *Imitations of Horace* show that he recognized that type of criticism which undertakes the historical development of a poetical kind. But he did not trouble to pursue it, or rather the occasion did not warrant the pursuit. Nor did he think it appropriate to make a considered statement in the *Lives* about what he looked for in poetry, though his demands are implicit in all he says.

He looked to poetry, as all neo-classical critics did, to give him both profit and pleasure, and was at one with Dennis in thinking that, though the end of poetry is moral, poetry will not improve us unless it has first attended to the subordinate aim of giving pleasure. And so he complains that the morality of *Cooper's Hill* is too frequent, that the Attendant Spirit's

moralizings in *Comus* are unacceptably presented—'the auditor
. . . listens as to a lecture, without passion, without anxiety'—
and that 'a long poem of mere sentiments easily becomes
tedious'. But what was it that pleased him? 'Smooth metre',
certainly, as he confesses in the 'Life of Pomfret'. Irregular
verse gave him no delight, for 'the great pleasure of verse', he
declares in the 'Life of Cowley', 'arises from the known measure
of the lines and uniform structure of the stanzas.' This accounts
for his displeasure with the verse of *Lycidas* and perhaps with
blank verse also; the rhythms were too uncertain. And poetry
did not entirely satisfy him unless it moved his passions.

He regrets that Waller is 'never pathetick, and very rarely
sublime', that Dryden 'with all his variety of excellence [is]
not often pathetick', and he rejoices that though there is little
opportunity for the pathetic in *Paradise Lost*, what little there
is has not been lost. But above all else the chief pleasure which
poetry could give him was a display of imagination or 'invention'. When poetic pleasure is mentioned by Johnson, the
reader usually finds it associated with one of these
qualities.

The definitions of poetry attempted in the Lives of Milton
and Waller imply this association. 'Poetry', Johnson writes,
in the first of those Lives, 'is the art of uniting pleasure with
truth, by calling imagination to the help of reason'; and in the
second of them, 'the essence of poetry is invention; such
invention as, by producing something unexpected, surprises
and delights'. The distinction between 'invention' and 'imagination' is explained in the 'Life of Pope', where we are told that
invention is the faculty 'by which new trains of events are
formed and new scenes of imagery displayed . . . and by which
extrinsick and adventitious embellishments and illustrations
are connected with a known subject', and that imagination is
that 'which strongly impresses on the writer's mind and enables
him to convey to the reader the various forms of nature,
incidents of life, and energies of passion'.

For Johnson, therefore, the poet is a creator by virtue of his
inventive and imaginative powers, and the evidence of that
creative ability is to be found in the poet's imagery. When

Johnson is pleased with a poet's work, his first words of commendation are usually given to the imagery. Thus Akenside's *Pleasures of Imagination* 'has undoubtedly a just claim to very particular notice as an example of great felicity of genius and uncommon amplitude of acquisitions, of a young mind stored with images, and much exercised in combining and comparing them'. Of *Comus* he writes that 'a work more truly poetical is rarely found', and in amplification of that judgment he immediately remarks that 'allusions, images, and descriptive epithets embellish almost every period with lavish decoration'. And the first quality of Gray's *Elegy* to attract his attention is that 'the *Church-yard* abounds with images which find a mirrour in every mind'.

The difference between Dryden's and Johnson's critical writing shows what changes had come about in criticism in the Augustan Age. Dryden's criticism is the criticism of an artist attempting to explain how his work was done. When he writes about Shakespeare or Jonson, Horace or Juvenal, he writes as a fellow-craftsman examining the work of other men confronted with similar problems; and he addresses a limited society of noble patrons, men whom he assumes to be his equals in culture, whose judgments are already formed. After Dryden's time critics, assuming a much wider audience, addressed themselves to the formation of the judgment; and perhaps it was in consequence that they began to inquire into the causes of poetic pleasure. We find these new inquiries started in the critical work of Dennis and Addison.

They attempted to give reasons for the pleasures they found in poetry and for the critical judgments they made. At their best they judge not by book but by reason. Rules there are, but the authority for those rules is to be found not in Aristotle but from where Aristotle himself drew them, 'from the bottom of the most profound philosophy, and the deepest knowledge of the heart of man'. It is in this tradition that Johnson worked. He was a poet, and no doubt his poetical experience assisted his criticism; but he did not write, like Dryden, as an artist examining another artist's methods. He wished to form his readers' judgments, to qualify their minds to think justly about poetry, and his appeal is therefore to the hearts and minds of his readers and not to the authority of books.[1]

What takes place in the hearts and minds of men was to Johnson of paramount interest; and that is characteristic of him, whether he is pointing out the 'inconvenience' of *Paradise Lost* that its plan 'comprises neither human actions nor human manners' or whether he is touring the Highlands with Boswell. He was by no means indifferent to the historical monuments of Scotland—his reflections on visiting Iona form the most notable passage of his *Journey to the Western Islands* (1775)— or to its scenery, but his business in visiting those remote regions was, he said, 'with life and manners'.

Page after page of that remarkable book is filled with the results of his inquiries into the smaller points of peasant economy—the value of the goat, the making of brogues, the use of seaweed for manure. He was never afraid that a detail might be too insignificant to mention, and the biographical sections of his *Lives of the Poets* are full of them. 'There is nothing, Sir, too little for so little a creature as man', he once said to Boswell; 'it is by studying little things that we attain the great art of having as little misery and as much happiness as possible'.[2] The same point is made in a letter Johnson wrote to Langton on the death of Peregrine Langton:

We must now endeavour to preserve what is left us,—his example of piety and œconomy. I hope you make what enquiries you can, and write down what is told you. The little things which distinguish domestick characters are soon forgotten: if you delay to enquire, you will have no information; if you neglect to write, information will be vain.

His art of life certainly deserves to be known and studied. He lived in plenty and elegance upon an income which, to many would appear indigent, and to most, scanty. How he lived, therefore, every man has an interest in knowing.[3]

[1]'The questions, whether the actions of the poem be strictly *one*, whether the poem can be properly termed *heroick* . . . are raised by such readers as draw their principles of judgement rather from books than from reason'. 'Life of Milton'.

[2]*Life*, ed. cit., i. 433.

[3]ibid., ii. 17.

Biography, then, has a moral purpose, even if the life is the life of a man little known to the world at large. It will teach men the art of living; it will serve the same purpose of mending the world which we have already seen informing the work of Addison, Swift, and Pope. Johnson's method here differed from the methods those writers had employed, but the object he has in view shows his kinship with the great Augustans.

CHAPTER X

CONCLUSION

THE further we proceed beyond the year 1760, the more remote seems the time of Dryden, Swift, and Pope. We find such men as Goldsmith, Johnson, and Chesterfield recognizing Pope and Dryden as classics of a former age; that in itself suggests that for better or for worse the Augustan Age was out, its achievements could be assessed, and that it was time to begin a new.

It is difficult to detect the moments of change in poetic taste and to measure the effect on contemporaries of books whose importance seems large in retrospect. But some signs of discontent can already be seen in Joseph Warton's poetry published in the seventeen-forties, and the need of a re-examination of judgments is implied in the first volume of Warton's *Essay on the Genius and Writings of Pope* (1756) and in Young's *Conjectures on Original Composition* (1759); but we can speak more confidently of shifting standards when we find Shenstone writing to his friend MacGowan in 1761:

The melody of our verse has been perhaps carried to its utmost perfection. . . . It seems to be a very favourable era for the appearance of such irregular poetry [as Macpherson's Erse fragments]. The taste of the age, so far as it regards plan and style, seems to have been carried to its utmost height, as may appear in the works of Akenside, Gray's Odes and Church-yard Verses, and Mason's Monody and Elfrida. The public has seen all that art can do, and they want the more striking efforts of wild, original, enthusiastic genius. It seems to exclaim aloud with the chorus in Julius Cæsar,

'Oh rather than be slaves to these deep learned men,
Give us our wildness and our woods, our huts and caves again!'

These were not the words of a young rebel or of an eccentric, they were the opinions of a man of forty-seven who had become

135

recognized as an arbiter of taste in his generation. The purpose of Shenstone's letter to MacGowan was to invite his friend's interest in 'a fair collection of the best old English and Scotch ballads' to be published by 'Mr. Percy . . . a man of learning, taste, and indefatigable industry'. The collection, Percy's *Reliques of Ancient English Poetry*, was not published until four years later (1765) when Shenstone was already dead; but while he lived, Shenstone took the keenest interest in Percy's work, and exercised a right of veto over the ballads chosen for publication.

Percy's own interests were mainly antiquarian, and in this aspect of the work he was abetted by Farmer, the great Elizabethan antiquary, and by Johnson, who may have suggested publication and who certainly wrote the dedication. In that dedication the nature of his and of Percy's interest is made unmistakably clear:

these poems are presented . . . not as labours of art, but as effusions of nature, shewing the first efforts of ancient genius, and exhibiting the customs and opinions of remote ages. . . . No active or comprehensive mind can forbear some attention to the reliques of antiquity: It is prompted by natural curiosity to survey the progress of life and manners, and to inquire by what gradations barbarity was civilized, grossness refined, and ignorance instructed.

It was Shenstone who insisted on keeping the balance. He was afraid that Percy's 'fondness for antiquity should tempt him to admit pieces that have no other sort of merit', and even that he might publish his ballads without the 'improvements' needed to render them acceptable to modern taste. But about the reception of the work, if Percy would only be sure to take his advice, he had no doubt whatever:

If I have any talent at Conjecture, All People of Taste, thro'out the Kingdom, will rejoice to see a judicious, a correct & elegant Collection of such Pieces. For after all, 'tis such Pieces, that contain yᵉ true *Chemical* Spirit or Essence of *Poetry;* a Little of which properly mingled is sufficient to strengthen & *keep alive* very considerable Quantities of the kind—Tis yᵉ *voice* of *Sentiment,* rather yⁿ the *Language* of *Reflexion;* adapted peculiarly to *strike* yᵉ

Passions, which is the only Merit of Poetry that has obtained my regard of late.[1]

This is not the language of Wordsworth, but these are the feelings with which Wordsworth regarded the *Reliques*: English poetry, he thought, had been 'absolutely redeemed by it'. But that was some fifty years later. We shall be disappointed if we expect to notice any immediate effect.

Percy was not the first to publish a selection of old ballads, and he was by no means the first to collect them. He knew of the collections made by Pepys and Anthony à Wood in the seventeenth century, and these were only some of the collections he drew upon, one of the most important being the folio manuscript he himself had found at a friend's house in Shropshire, 'lying dirty on the floor under a bureau in the parlour, being used by the maids to light the fire'. His work, in fact, may be said to have set the seal of scholarship on much former dilettantism.

The scholarship, indeed, is even more evident in Percy's treatment of the Elizabethan lyrics which he interspersed amongst the old ballads so as 'to take off from the tediousness of the longer narratives'; for while, in editing the ballads, Percy followed the customary practice of adapting minor poetry of the past to suit the taste of the time[2], he took the greatest pains to secure the best available texts of the Elizabethan lyrics. Any reader of the *Reliques* who was fond of songs would have been familiar with most of the lyrics Percy printed, for

[1]Shenstone to Percy, 10th November, 1760; *Letters*, ed. Williams (1939), p. 564.

[2]'The Editor has endeavoured to be as faithful as the imperfect state of his materials would admit. For these old popular rhymes being many of them copied only from illiterate transcripts, or the imperfect recitation of itinerant ballad-singers, have, as might be expected, been handed down to us with less care than any other writings in the world. And the old copies, whether manuscript or printed, were often so defective or corrupted, that a scrupulous adherence to their wretched readings would only have exhibited unintelligible nonsense, or such poor meagre stuff as neither came from the Bard nor was worthy of the Press: when, by a few slight corrections or additions, a most beautiful or interesting sense hath started forth, and this so naturally and easily, that the Editor could seldom prevail on himself to indulge the vanity of making a formal claim to the improvement. . . .' From Percy's preface.

they had appeared time and again in modernized form in the song books of the day[1]; but this was the first time they had appeared in their original freshness, a freshness and *naïveté* which they seemed to share with the ballads around them.

It was, therefore, upon the merit of his scholarship that Percy principally rested; but he hoped to please 'the reader of taste' as well as 'the judicious antiquary' and to 'gratify both without offending either'. The sales of the book show that Percy succeeded, for as many as seven editions and reprints were required within the next thirty years. Furthermore the reviewers were favourably impressed.

The Monthly Review devoted twelve and a half pages to the book and thanked Percy for 'a very elegant, instructive, and entertaining compilation'; and as for the ballads, the reviewer was 'far from thinking with certain tasteless Readers that there is no merit in the Compositions themselves; on the contrary, we find in many of them that pleasing simplicity & those artless graces, which . . . compensate for the want of superior beauties'. The tone is condescending, and the standard by which the ballads are being tried is neo-classical; but the reviewer has detected those graces of simplicity which Shenstone admired and which lie beyond the reach of art.

This artless simplicity of sentiment and diction was evidently what made the greatest impression on the first readers of the *Reliques*, but we cannot suppose that they were not also aware of a freshness of subject matter. When Percy remarked to Warton in 1762 that the public 'seems to loath all common forms of Poetry; & requires some new species to quicken its pall'd appetite', Warton agreed and added that what the public wants is 'Poetry endued with new Manners & new Images'. New manners and new images were what the *Reliques* supplied.

Apart from a few poems like Gray's 'Bard', the subject matter of eighteenth-century poetry had been contemporary: it had reflected the manners and the thought of the time. Through Percy's ballads and his scholarly apparatus, readers could now escape into an old and strange world of less sophisti-

[1]Evidence will be found in Earl R. Wasserman, *Elizabethan Poetry in the Eighteenth Century* (Urbana, Ill., 1947), ch. iv.

cated thoughts and manners. It was a world to which a few scholars and ballad-collectors already had access. Readers of Spenser could see it through the eyes of an Elizabethan; and Richard Hurd in his *Letters on Chivalry and Romance* (1761) had expounded its customs. But now this world was open to the reader as it had never been open before.

The effect of this new enthusiasm for the Middle Ages upon the architecture and the novels of the time must be left for someone else to relate. The effect upon poetry was to stimulate poets to live once more in a world of their own imagining. We see Chatterton attempting this in his Rowley poems within a few years of the publication of the *Reliques*. The youngster was not well informed about medieval England and he knew little either of its language or of its literature, though that did not affect the vividness of the Middle Ages he imagined. But if we want to find the Middle Ages more accurately re-created we must look at the learned Thomas Warton's odes, *The Crusade* and *The Grave of King Arthur* (1777), and then much further ahead to Scott.

It is in Scott's poems, and more particularly in *The Ancient Mariner* and *La Belle Dame Sans Merci*, that we see what Wordsworth meant when he declared that English poetry had been absolutely redeemed by the *Reliques*, for in those poems, though in differing degrees, we find both the simplicity of sentiment and of diction and the new manners and new images which the *Reliques* presented.

But this naked simplicity might well have been found in more and more poems even if Percy had never published his *Reliques*. We have already seen Shenstone welcoming the coming publication of the *Reliques* just because it seemed in tune with his own attempts in poetry. 'Were I rich', he writes on one occasion[1], 'I would erect a Temple to *Simplicity* and *Grace*', and on another[2] 'My chief endeavour . . . has been to produce *ease* & Simplicity, if not melody of expression, so far as this c^d be effected without *impoverishing* the Sentiment . . . Pastoral Poetry, in my opinion, should exhibit almost naked sentiment'.

[1] To Dodsley, 20th November, 1762; *Letters*, p. 642.
[2] To Percy, January, 1762; *Letters*, p. 616.

His shorter poems at best are more often graceful than
simple, but he exhibits the naked sentiment just often enough
for us to appreciate the ideal he set himself. If his notion of
simplicity, like Beattie's, 'discards everything from style, which
is affected, superfluous, indefinite, or obscure, but admits
every grace, which, without encumbering a sentiment, does
really embellish and enforce it',[1] then we may say that these
lines from his *Pastoral Ballad* are 'simple':

> She gaz'd, as I slowly withdrew;
>   My path I could hardly discern;
> So sweetly she bade me adieu,
>   I thought that she bade me return.

In the years ahead more and more poets were to exhibit a
simplicity and nakedness of sentiment and to touch the breast
of the Man of Feeling with melancholy reflections. Goldsmith's
song in *The Vicar of Wakefield*, 'When lovely woman stoops to
folly' and Cowper's 'The Shrubbery' are beautifully restrained
examples; and for at least one reader the sonnets of Bowles
were found tender and yet manly, natural and real and yet
dignified and harmonious.[2]

Cowper, indeed, would scarcely have gone so far as to agree
with Shenstone that 'the voice of sentiment (rather than the
language of reflexion), peculiarly adapted to strike the passions,
is the only merit of poetry'; but, if we may trust Marianne
Dashwood,[3] it was the voice of sentiment to which readers of
his poetry listened. And they could be sure that it was Cowper's
own voice they heard, speaking directly of his own experiences.
He was the 'stricken deer, that left the herd long since'; it was
his 'panting side' that was 'with many an arrow deep infix'd';
it was he that was 'whelm'd in deeper gulphs' than the castaway.
It is true that some of the most prominent Augustans, notably
Pope, Swift, and Prior, had formerly written of their own
emotions; but more recently it had been felt that a greater
propriety was shown in concealing the individuality of the

[1]In a letter to Forbes, 30th January, 1766; W. Forbes, *Life of Beattie*
(1806; ed. of 1824, i. 69).

[2]See Coleridge, *Biographia Literaria*, ch. 1.

[3]See Jane Austen, *Sense and Sensibility*, ch. iv.

sentiment. For the most part, it is not Thomson himself but Man or the Poet who observes and feels in *The Seasons*, and when Collins mourns for Thomson's death it is 'Remembrance' that

> oft shall haunt the Shore
> When THAMES in Summer-wreaths is drest,
> And oft suspend the dashing Oar
> To bid his gentle Spirit rest!

And when Gray speaks in his own person in the second stanza of the 'Ode on a Distant Prospect of Eton College' he endeavours to represent the feelings of every man in a similar state. But in the last thirty years of the century there was much less hesitation in inviting response to individual sentiment. That was what Cowper offered, and what Beattie before him had offered, a little diffidently, in *The Minstrel* (1771). Beattie, indeed, was surprised at the enthusiastic reception given to his poem:

the sentiments, expressed in the Minstrel [he wrote], being not common to all men, but peculiar to persons of a certain cast, cannot possibly be interesting, because the generality of readers will not understand nor feel them so thoroughly as to think them natural. That a boy should take pleasure in darkness or a storm . . . should be more gratified with listening to music at a distance, than with mixing in the merriment occasioned by it . . . [sentiments which] would be natural to persons of a certain cast, will be condemned as unnatural by others, who have never felt them in themselves, nor observed them in the generality of mankind. Of all this I was sufficiently aware before I published the Minstrel, and, therefore, never expected that it would be a popular poem.[1]

But Beattie had reckoned without the change in taste. His disguise as the minstrel Edwin was soon penetrated and the best judges were charmed. Mrs. Montagu, the Queen of the Bluestockings and a great admirer of Beattie, accounted for the poem's success with the following generalization, which points to the recent change in taste:

General reflections, natural sentiments, representations of the passions, are things addressed to the understanding. A poet should

[1]*Life*, ed.cit., i. 197.

aim at touching the heart. Strong sympathies are to be excited, and deep impressions only to be made, by interesting us for an individual.[1]

As we read these requests for 'new Manners and new Images', for 'naked sentiment', for what will touch the heart by its record of the individual, for a simplicity of style which discards whatever is 'affected, superfluous, indefinite, or obscure', we gain the impression that critical demand has momentarily outstepped poetic supply. Supply was to be rapidly increased in the last decade of the century with the first volumes of Rogers, Wordsworth, Coleridge, Southey, and Campbell, and readers uncorrupted by political prejudice might at last see in the best of this new work the prospect of their demands being shortly fulfilled.

[1]op.cit., p. 187.

NOTES FOR
FURTHER READING

NOTES FOR FURTHER READING

CHAPTER I. The standard library edition of Dryden's poems is by James Kinsley in four volumes (Oxford, 1958) and there is a one-volume version, excluding the translation of Virgil, in the Oxford Standard Authors series (1962). The one-volume edition by G. R. Noyes (Cambridge, Mass., revd. 1950) not only contains the translation of Virgil but still has much to commend it as an annotated text. The California edition of *The Works*, in course of publication, is planned on a much more massive scale than the Oxford edition.

The standard life of Dryden is by Charles E. Ward (Durham, North Carolina, 1961).

The best short introduction to Dryden's career is Bonamy Dobrée's *John Dryden* in the British Council's 'Writers and Their Work' series (1956), and the best short assessment of his quality as a poet is James Sutherland's *John Dryden: The Poet as Orator* (Glasgow, 1963). The most sympathetic study of Dryden's poetic craftsmanship is Mark Van Doren's *John Dryden: A Study of his Poetry* (New York, 1920), of which an English edition was published in 1931 and a revised American edition in 1946. This was the book which provoked T. S. Eliot's famous review, later reprinted as *Homage to John Dryden* (London, 1924), and was followed by his *John Dryden: The Poet, The Dramatist, The Critic* (New York, 1932). There are good chapters on Dryden's satires in Ian Jack's *Augustan Satire* (Oxford, 1952); his dramatic work is studied in Bonamy Dobrée's *Restoration Comedy* (Oxford, 1924) and *Restoration Tragedy* (Oxford, 1930), K. M. Lynch's *The Social Mode of Restoration Comedy* (New York, 1926) and C. V. Deane's *Dramatic Theory and the Rhymed Heroic Play* (London, 1931). Still the best survey of Dryden's prose writings is W. P. Ker's introduction to his selection (Oxford, 1900). The philosophical background of Dryden's work is examined in Louis I. Bredvold's *The Intellectual Milieu of John Dryden* (Ann Arbor, 1934). Hugh Macdonald's *John Dryden: A Bibliography of Early Editions and Drydeniana* (Oxford, 1939) is an essential book of reference.

It is invidious to chose between the numerous specialized articles on various aspects of Dryden's work, but the following will be found particularly helpful: R. F. Jones, 'The originality of *Absalom and Achitophel*', *Mod. Lang. Notes*, xlvi, 1931; Ernest Brenacke, Jr., 'Dryden's Odes and Draghi's Music', *Publications of the Mod. Lang. Assoc. of America*, 1934; Edward N. Hooker. 'The purpose of Dryden's *Annus Mirabilis*', *Huntington Library Quarterly*, x, 1946.

CHAPTER II. For further study of subjects discussed in this chapter, see Basil Willey, *Seventeenth-Century Background* (London, 1934), and his *Eighteenth-Century Background* (London, 1940); Arthur O. Lovejoy, '"Pride" in Eighteenth-Century Thought' and 'The Parallel of Deism and Classicism', reprinted in his *Essays in the History of Ideas* (Baltimore, 1948); R. F. Jones, 'The Background of *The Battle of the Books*', reprinted in his *The Seventeenth Century* (Stanford, 1951); essays by Arthur O. Lovejoy and Louis I. Bredvold in *Eighteenth-Century English Literature: Modern Essays in Criticism*, ed. James L. Clifford (Oxford University Press, 1959).

CHAPTER III. The best life of Addison is by Peter Smithers (Oxford, 1954), and there are critical estimates by Bonamy Dobrée in *Essays in Biography: 1680–1726* (Oxford, 1925) and by C. S. Lewis in *Eighteenth-Century English Literature* (cited above). Walter Graham, who edited Addison's not very interesting letters (Oxford, 1941), wrote the best account of the journalistic background of *The Tatler* in *The Beginnings of English Literary Periodicals* (London, 1926).

Edward N. Hooker's edition of Dennis's critical works (Baltimore, 1939, 1943) reinstated Dennis as a critic, and his introduction is indispensable for the study of neo-classical theories of criticism.

Hurd's *Letters on Chivalry and Romance* have been edited by Hoyt Trowbridge, whose essay 'Bishop Hurd: a reinterpretation', *Publications of the Mod. Lang. Assoc. of America*, lviii, 1943 is important. See also Arthur Johnston, *Enchanted Ground*, ch. 2 (London, 1964), and for Addison's ballad criticism Albert B. Friedman, *The Ballad Revival*, ch. 4 (Chicago, 1961).

CHAPTER IV. The most valuable help in the study of Swift is to be found in the introduction and notes to the editions of his writings published mostly during the last twenty-five years; notably *A Tale of a Tub*, ed. A. C. Guthkelch and D. Nichol Smith (Oxford; revd. ed., 1958), *The Drapier Letters*, ed. Herbert Davis (Oxford, 1935), *The Letters of Jonathan Swift to Charles Ford*, ed. D. Nichol Smith (Oxford, 1935), Swift's *Poems*, ed. Harold Williams (Oxford; revd. ed., 1958), *A Journal to Stella*, ed. Harold Williams (Oxford, 1948), and Herbert Davis's edition of Swift's prose works to be completed in 14 volumes, which began to appear in 1941. A new edition of his *Correspondence*, ed. Harold Williams, in six volumes is in course of publication (Oxford, 1963).

The first volume of a new biography by Irvin Ehrenpreis, *Swift: the Man, his Works, and the Age*, has been published (London, 1962).

The best introductions to Swift are R. Quintana's *The Mind and Art of Jonathan Swift* (New York, 1936; London, 1953), and his *Swift: an Introduction* (London, 1955). Kathleen Williams's *Jonathan Swift and the Age of Compromise* (Constable, 1959) is also recommended.

In addition to the essays in *Eighteenth-Century English Literature* (see under Chapter II), the following books and articles will be found useful on specific aspects of Swift's work: E. Pons, *Swift: les Années de Jeunesse et le Conte du Tonneau* (Strasburg, 1925); R. F. Jones, *Ancients and Moderns* (St. Louis, 1936) on the background of *The Battle of the Books;* Sir Charles Firth, 'The Political Significance of *Gulliver's Travels*' (1919; reprinted in his *Essays Historical and Literary*, Oxford, 1938); Marjorie Nicolson and Nora M. Mohler, 'The Scientific Background of Swift's Voyage to Laputa', *Annals of*

Science, II, 1937; Arthur E. Case, *Four Essays on Gulliver's Travels* (Princeton, 1945); Louis A. Landa, 'Swift, the Mysteries, and Deism', *Texas Studies in English*, 1944; Miriam K. Starkman, *Swift's Satire on Learning in 'A Tale of a Tub'* (Princeton, 1950); George Sherburn, 'Errors concerning the Houyhnhnms', *Modern Philology*, lvi, 1958; R. S. Crane, 'The Houyhnhnms, the Yahoos, and the History of Ideas', in *Reason and the Imagination*, ed. J. A. Mazzeo (London, 1962).

CHAPTER V. As with Swift, so with the study of Pope, help will be found in the 'Twickenham' edition of his poems (6 vols., London, 1939–61; one-volume version, 1963). His *Correspondence* is edited by G. Sherburn (5 vols., Oxford, 1956); there is a selection in World's Classics, 1959.

In *The Early Career of Alexander Pope* (Oxford, 1934) George Sherburn carried the biography of Pope down to 1727; more biographical details will be found in Norman Ault's *New Light on Pope* (London, 1950). The best short life is Bonamy Dobrée's *Alexander Pope* (London, 1951).

In addition to the essays in *Eighteenth-Century English Literature* (see under Chapter II), the following will be found useful: Geoffrey Tillotson, *On the Poetry of Pope* (Oxford, 1938) and his *Pope and Human Nature* (Oxford, 1958); Aubrey L. Williams, *Pope's Dunciad: A Study of its Meaning* (London, 1955); Reuben A. Brower, *Alexander Pope: The Poetry of Allusion* (Oxford, 1959); *Essential Articles for the Study of Alexander Pope*, ed. Maynard Mack (Hamden, Connecticut, 1964).

CHAPTER VI. The understanding of Thomson's poetry has been greatly advanced by four American scholars: C. A. Moore in his 'Shaftesbury and the Ethical Poets in England, 1700–1760', *Publications of the Mod. Lang. Assoc. of America*, xxxi, 1916, Herbert Drennon in his 'Scientific Rationalism and James Thomson's Poetic Art', *Stud. in Philology*, xxxi, 1934, A. D. McKillop, *The Background of Thomson's Seasons* (Minneapolis, 1942), and Marjorie Nicolson, *Newton demands the Muse* (Princeton, 1946). There is a life of Thomson by Douglas Grant

(London, 1951). See also Ralph Cohen's important study of the criticism of Thomson, *The Art of Discrimination* (London, 1964).

Contemporary theories of the Sublime may be studied in Samuel H. Monk's *The Sublime: A Study of Critical Theories in Eighteenth-Century England* (New York, 1935).

CHAPTER VII. R. D. Havens, *The Influence of Milton on English Poetry* (Cambridge, U.S.A., 1922); Geoffrey Tillotson *Essays in Criticism and Research* (Cambridge, 1942), and his *Augustan Studies* (London, 1961); W. L. Renwick, 'Notes on some lesser poets of the Eighteenth Century', *Essays on the Eighteenth Century presented to David Nichol Smith* (Oxford, 1945); James Sutherland, *A Preface to Eighteenth-Century Poetry* (Oxford, 1948); J. W. Mackail, 'Edward Young', *Studies of English Poets* (London, 1926); H. W. Garrod, *Collins* (Oxford, 1928); A. S. P. Woodhouse, 'Collins and the Creative Imagination', *Studies in English by Members of University College, Toronto* (Toronto, 1931); E. G. Ainsworth, *Poor Collins* (Ithaca, 1937); A. R. Humphreys, *William Shenstone* (Cambridge, 1937). See also the excellent edition of Thomson's *Castle of Indolence* (and other poems) by A. D. McKillop (Lawrence, Kansas, 1961).

CHAPTER VIII. Gray's first biographer, his friend Mason, made Gray's letters the basis of his memoir (1775), and the letters will inevitably remain our most important commentary upon the man and his poetry. The most complete and worthy edition is by Paget Toynbee and Leonard Whibley (Oxford, 1935). The best life of Gray is by R. W. Ketton-Cremer (Cambridge, 1955). There is much information to be gleaned from D. C. Tovey's edition of *Gray's English Poems* (Cambridge, 1898) and from F. G. Stokes's edition of the *Elegy* (Oxford, 1929), and much pleasure to be derived from Lord David Cecil's *The Poetry of Thomas Gray* (London, 1945). See also E. D. Snyder, *The Celtic Revival in English Literature: 1760–1800* (Cambridge, Mass., 1923), A. L. Reed, *The Background of Gray's Elegy* (New York, 1924), Cleanth Brooks's study of the *Elegy* in his *The Well Wrought Urn* (New York, 1947), and Geoffrey Tillotson, *Augustan Studies* (London, 1961).

CHAPTER IX. Boswell's *Life of Johnson*, of which the standard edition is by G. B. Hill, revised by L. F. Powell (6 vols., Oxford, 1934–50) may be supplemented with other contemporary accounts and memoirs, of which G. B. Hill's *Johnsonian Miscellanies* (Oxford, 1897) is a convenient collection. The best modern lives are by J. W. Krutch (New York, 1944; London, 1948), and by James L. Clifford, *Young Samuel Johnson* (London, 1955). The best general studies are Sir Walter Raleigh's *Six Essays on Johnson* (Oxford, 1910), D. Nichol Smith's 'Johnson and Boswell', *Cambridge History of English Literature*, vol. x, 1913, Bertrand H. Bronson's *Johnson Agonistes* (Cambridge, 1946), W. J. Bate's *The Achievement of Samuel Johnson* (London, 1955), and M. J. C. Hodgart's *Samuel Johnson and his Times* (London, 1962).

In addition to essays in *Eighteenth-Century English Literature* (see under Chapter II) and *New Light on Dr. Johnson*, ed. F. W. Hilles (New Haven, 1959), the following books and articles will be found useful: Sir Walter Raleigh's introduction to *Johnson on Shakespeare* (Oxford, 1908), and D. Nichol Smith's *Shakespeare in the Eighteenth Century* (Oxford, 1928); J. H. Hagstrum, *Samuel Johnson's Literary Criticism* (London, 1952); D. T. Starnes and G. E. Noyes, *The English Dictionary from Cawdrey to Johnson* (Chapel Hill, 1946); James H. Sledd and Gwin J. Kolb, *Dr. Johnson's Dictionary* (Chicago, 1955); Donald J. Greene, *The Politics of Samuel Johnson* (New Haven, 1960); Bergen Evans 'Dr. Johnson's Theory of Poetry', *Review of English Studies*, x, 1934, Mary Lascelles, '*Rasselas* Reconsidered', *Essays and Studies* (London, 1951), and Benjamin Boyce, 'Samuel Johnson's Criticism of Pope', *ibid.*, n.s., v, 1954.

CHAPTER X. Cleanth Brooks, 'The Country Parson as Research Scholar', *Publications of the Bibliographical Society of America*, liii, 1959, provides the best short survey of Percy's career. For studies of his *Reliques*, see *The Ballad Revival*, ch. 7 and *Enchanted Ground*, ch. 3, both cited under Chapter III.

INDEX

INDEX

[Principal entries are represented in bold type]

153

In the Norton Library

CRITICISM AND THE HISTORY OF IDEAS

Norton Critical Editions

Inexpensive paperbacks containing authoritative texts, carefully annotated, plus comprehensive selections of criticism and source materials.

IN PREPARATION